BEGINNERS GUIDE TO SELL ON ETSY WITH TIKTOK

INNOVATIVE STRATEGIES TO SELL CRAFTS AND ANTIQUES ONLINE TO MAKE PASSIVE INCOME

FRANKLIN OWEN

COPYRIGHT

Reservation of rights. Except for brief extracts from those used in critical reviews and for non-commercial uses permitted by copyright law, no part of this publication may be reproduced, distributed, or broadcast in any form without the prior written consent of the publisher. This prohibition includes photocopying, recording and other electronic or mechanical means.

Copyright © FRANKLIN OWEN, 2024.

TABLE OF CONTENT

COPYRIGHT	2
TABLE OF CONTENT	3
INTRODUCTION	8
CHAPTER 1: :GETTING STARTED WITH ETSY	12
SETTING UP YOUR ETSY SHOP	12
CRAFTING YOUR BRAND IDENTITY	17
ESSENTIAL TOOLS AND RESOURCES	21
CHAPTER 2: UNDERSTANDING YOUR MARKET	25
IDENTIFYING YOUR NICHE	25
FINDING YOUR UNIQUE SELLING PROPOSITION	32
CHAPTER 3:CREATING CRAFT PRODUCTS THAT SELL	37
PRODUCT DEVELOPMENT TIPS	37
CRAFTING HIGH-QUALITY ITEMS	40
PRICING STRATEGIES FOR MAXIMUM PROFIT	44
CHAPTER 4: OPTIMIZING YOUR ETSY LISTINGS	51
CRAFTING COMPELLING TITLES AND DESCRIPTIONS	51
THE IMPORTANCE OF KEYWORDS AND SEO	54
USING HIGH-QUALITY IMAGES AND VIDEOS	57
Chapter 5: Mastering Etsy Shop Management	63

MANAGING ORDERS AND INVENTORY	63
CUSTOMER SERVICE EXCELLENCE	67
Handling Returns	70
HANDLING COMPLAINTS	72

CHAPTER 6:INTRODUCTION TO TIKTOK FOR BUSINESS — 76

SETTING UP YOUR TIK TOK PROFILE	76
NAVIGATING TIKTOK'S INTERFACE	81

CHAPTER 7:INTRODUCTION TO TIKTOK FOR BUSINESS — 87

UNDERSTANDING TIKTOK'S ALGORITHM	87
User Interactions	88
Watch Time And Completion Rate	88
Replays	89
Shares	89
Comments	90
Likes	90
Video Information	91

CHAPTER 8:CREATING ENGAGING TIKTOK CONTENT — 96

TYPES OF VIDEOS THAT DRIVE SALES	96
Product Showcases	96
Behind-the-scenes Videos	97
Customer Testimonials And Reviews	98
Tutorials And How-to Videos	99
Unboxing And Haul Videos	99
Trend-Based Content	100
THE POWER OF TIKTOK TRENDS AND CHALLENGES	100

4

CRAFTING A CONTENT CALENDAR	106

CHAPTER 9: TIKTOK MARKETING STRATEGIES 116

LEVERAGING HASHTAGS AND MUSIC	116
The Power of Hashtags	116
Harnessing the Emotional Power of Music	118
Combining Hashtags and Music for Maximum Impact	119
USING TIKTOK ADS	120
Measuring and Optimizing Ad Performance	124
COLLABORATIONS AND INFLUENCER MARKETING	126

CHAPTER 10: BUILDING YOUR BRAND ON TIKTOK 132

ESTABLISHING YOUR BRAND VOICE	132
ENGAGING WITH YOUR AUDIENCE	134
GROWING YOUR FOLLOWER BASE	141

CHAPTER 11: LINKING TIKTOK TO YOUR ETSY SHOP 146

ADDING CLICKABLE LINKS	146
CREATING EFFECTIVE CALL-TO-ACTIONS	148
USING TIKTOK ANALYTICS TO IMPROVE PERFORMANCE	152
Understanding TikTok Analytics	152
Overview Section	153
Content Section	154
Followers Section	155
USING INSIGHTS TO IMPROVE PERFORMANCE	156

CHAPTER 11: CONVERTING TIKTOK TRAFFIC TO ETSY SALES 160

INTEGRATING TIKTOK CONTENT WITH ETSY LISTINGS	**160**
Bridging the Gap Between TikTok and Etsy	160
Showcasing Products on TikTok	161
Creating a Seamless Transition	162
Enhancing Etsy Listings with TikTok Content	163
Leveraging TikTok Trends and Hashtags	164
Engaging with Your Audience	164
Optimizing the Customer Journey	165
Analyzing and Refining Your Strategy	166
Building Long-Term Relationships	166
SHOWCASING PRODUCT FEATURES AND BENEFITS	167
USING TIKTOK STORIES FOR PROMOTIONS	170
CHAPTER 13: ADVANCED TIKTOK TECHNIQUES FOR ETSY SELLERS	**174**
USING USER-GENERATED CONTENT	**174**
CHAPTER 14: EXPANDING YOUR REACH BEYOND TIKTOK	**177**
CROSS-PROMOTING ON OTHER SOCIAL MEDIA PLATFORMS	**177**
EMAIL MARKETING TIPS	180
PAID ADVERTISING STRATEGIES	183
CHAPTER 14: SCALING YOUR ETSY BUSINESS WITH TIKTOK	**185**
OUTSOURCING AND HIRING HELP	185
EXPANDING PRODUCT LINES	187
EXPLORING WHOLESALE OPPORTUNITIES	189
CONCLUSION	**192**

YOUR JOURNEY TO SIX FIGURES AND BEYOND 192
    FINAL TIPS AND ENCOURAGEMENT 193
RESOURCES FOR ONGOING SUPPORT 195

INTRODUCTION

Welcome to a world brimming with opportunities, where your passion for crafting can blossom into a thriving business. If you're holding this book, it's because you have a dream—to transform your love for creating handmade items into a successful venture that not only brings joy to others but also generates a significant income. You've likely heard of countless artisans making six figures by selling their unique creations online and wondered how you could achieve the same. You're in the right place.

This guide, "BEGINNERS GUIDE TO SELL ON ETSY WITH TIKTOK: Etsy Hidden Secrets For Beginners To Make Six Figures By Selling Crafts Online," is crafted with you in mind. Whether you are a complete novice stepping into the world of online selling or someone who has tried their hand at it but hasn't yet found the success you desire, this book is your key to unlocking that potential. We will walk you through every step, from setting up your Etsy shop to mastering the art of TikTok marketing.

Etsy, the renowned marketplace for handmade and vintage goods, offers a platform where creativity thrives. It has opened doors for countless creators, allowing their talents to reach a global audience. However, in a marketplace filled with talented artisans, standing out can be challenging. This is where TikTok becomes your secret weapon. TikTok, the fast-growing social media platform, is not just a hub for viral dance challenges and funny videos; it's a powerful marketing tool that can elevate your Etsy shop to new heights. Its algorithm favors creative, engaging content, providing you with a unique opportunity to showcase your products and connect with potential customers in a way that feels genuine and exciting.

There are numerous resources available that cover either Etsy or TikTok, but few delve into how to combine the strengths of both platforms to maximize your business potential. This book fills that gap, offering you a comprehensive guide to using both worlds. We will start by helping you set up and optimize your Etsy shop, ensuring that your brand identity is clear and compelling. You will learn how to research your market, identify your niche, and create products that captivate buyers. Crafting compelling listings that draw in customers is an art, and we will guide you through the process, emphasizing the importance of keywords, high-quality images, and engaging descriptions.

Once your Etsy shop is ready, we will shift our focus to TikTok. You will discover how to set up your profile, understand the platform's algorithm, and create content that resonates with your target audience. TikTok is all about creativity and engagement. We will explore different types of videos that can drive sales, how to leverage trending challenges, and the importance of a well-thought-out content calendar. Building your brand on TikTok involves more than just posting videos; it's about establishing a voice, engaging with your audience, and growing a loyal follower base.

As you create engaging TikTok content, you will learn how to link it effectively to your Etsy shop. We will cover everything from adding clickable links to creating compelling call-to-actions and using analytics to fine-tune your strategy. Converting TikTok followers into loyal Etsy customers requires a seamless integration of your content with your product listings, and we will show you how to make this transition smooth and effective.

Beyond TikTok, we will delve into other marketing strategies to expand your reach. From cross-promoting on other social media platforms to utilizing email marketing and paid advertising, you will have a toolkit of strategies to ensure your business grows steadily. Scaling your Etsy business involves more than just increasing sales; it's about managing your finances wisely, exploring wholesale opportunities, and continuously adapting to market trends.

Selling on Etsy and leveraging TikTok is not just about making money. It's about sharing your art with the world, building a brand that people connect with, and creating a community around your passion. Success in this journey doesn't come overnight. It requires dedication, creativity, and a willingness to learn and adapt. This book is your roadmap, filled with actionable insights, practical tips, and real-world examples to guide you every step of the way.

So, are you ready to turn your crafting dreams into reality? Let's dive in and unlock the hidden secrets of selling on Etsy with TikTok, paving your way to six-figure success and beyond

CHAPTER 1: :GETTING STARTED WITH ETSY

SETTING UP YOUR ETSY SHOP

Imagine stepping into a vast, bustling marketplace filled with eager shoppers searching for unique, handmade treasures. This is Etsy, a platform where creativity meets commerce, offering you the chance to turn your passion into profit. Setting up your Etsy shop is the first crucial step on this exciting journey. While it may seem daunting at first, the process is straightforward and, dare I say, enjoyable. Let's dive in and explore every nook and cranny of setting up your Etsy shop.

First things first, you'll need to create an account. If you already have an Etsy account as a buyer, you're halfway there. Simply log in and navigate to the "Sell on Etsy" option. If you're new to Etsy, head over to Etsy.com and click "Register" to get started. You'll be asked for basic information such as your name, email address, and a password. Once you've confirmed your email, you're ready to start setting up your shop.

Now, let's talk about your shop name. This is more important than you might think. Your shop name is the first impression potential buyers will have of your brand. It needs to be memorable, easy to spell, and reflect what you sell. Spend some time brainstorming ideas. Think about words that represent your products, your style, and your personality. You might want to jot down a few possibilities and see how they look and feel. Once you've settled on the perfect name, check its availability on Etsy. If it's already taken, don't worry, you can get creative with variations until you find the right one.

With your shop name in place, it's time to start building the bones of your shop. Etsy will guide you through a series of steps, starting with your shop preferences. Here, you'll choose your shop's language, country, and currency. This helps Etsy tailor your shop's interface and information to your specific needs. It's straightforward, but it's also a critical step, ensuring your shop is accessible and user-friendly.

Next, you'll set up your shop's visual identity, starting with your shop banner and logo. Think of these as the storefront of your online shop. They should be inviting and clearly convey what your shop is about. If you're not a graphic designer, don't fret. There are plenty of online tools like Canva that offer user-friendly templates you can customize to create professional-looking graphics. Your banner should be 3360 x 840 pixels for optimal display. Keep it simple, clean, and reflective of your brand.

Your shop logo, on the other hand, should be 500 x 500 pixels. This is the icon that will represent your shop across Etsy, so it should be something that stands out and is easily recognizable. If you have a logo already, great! If not, consider using your shop name in a unique font or design that captures the essence of your brand.

Once your visuals are set, it's time to write your shop's "About" section. This is your chance to tell your story. Shoppers on Etsy love to know the person behind the product. Why did you start crafting? What inspires you? What is unique about your process or materials? Be genuine and let your personality shine through. This isn't just about selling products; it's about connecting with your customers and building a loyal following.

After your "About" section, you'll want to move on to your shop policies. This might sound dry, but it's essential for setting clear expectations with your customers. Outline your policies on shipping, returns, and exchanges. Be transparent about your processing times and shipping costs. The more information you provide upfront, the less room there is for misunderstandings and disputes later on. Think about the questions you would have as a buyer and answer them in your policies.

Now, we get to the heart of your shop—your product listings. This is where you get to showcase your creations to the world. Each listing should be as detailed and enticing as possible. Start with your product photos. These are arguably the most crucial part of your listing. Clear, high-quality photos can make all the difference in attracting buyers. Use natural light and multiple angles to capture your product from every perspective. Include close-ups of any unique features or details.

Your main photo should be the one that grabs attention in search results. Make sure it's well-lit, sharp, and shows the product in its best light. The additional photos can provide more context and show the product in use. If you sell clothing or accessories, consider using models to show how the items look when worn. For home decor or art, show the product in a styled setting.

After your photos, the product title is the next critical element. It needs to be descriptive and include keywords that potential buyers might use when searching for similar items. Think about the main features of your product and use those in the title. For example, instead of just saying "Bracelet," you could say "Handmade Beaded Bracelet with Natural Stones." This not only tells the buyer what the product is but also helps with Etsy's search algorithm.

The description is your chance to dive deeper into the details. Start with a brief, engaging overview of the product. Then, provide specifics: size, materials, care instructions, and any unique features. Use bullet points to make the information easy to scan. Be honest and clear; if there are any imperfections or variations due to the handmade nature of the product, mention them. This builds trust with your customers.

Next, you'll set your price. Pricing can be tricky, but it's crucial to get it right. Consider the cost of materials, your time, and any other expenses like shipping and Etsy fees. Look at what similar items are selling for and position your price competitively. Don't undervalue your work; handmade items are unique and often worth more than mass-produced products.

With your product details in place, you'll move on to tags. These are keywords that help buyers find your products in Etsy's search. Think about what words or phrases a buyer might use when looking for your item and include those as tags. You can use up to 13 tags, so make them count.

Shipping is another vital aspect of your listings. Decide whether you'll offer free shipping or charge based on the buyer's location. Be clear about your shipping times and methods. Offering free shipping can be a great incentive for buyers, but make sure to factor the cost into your pricing. Use Etsy's shipping calculator to estimate costs accurately and avoid any surprises.

Once you've filled in all the details, it's time to hit "Publish." Congratulations! Your product is now live on Etsy. But your work doesn't stop here. Promoting your shop is key to driving traffic and sales. Share your listings on social media, participate in Etsy teams and forums, and consider using Etsy's paid advertising options to boost your visibility.

Remember, setting up your Etsy shop is just the beginning. It's an ongoing process of refining your listings, experimenting with different strategies, and continuously learning and adapting. Pay attention to what works and what doesn't, and don't be afraid to make changes. Your Etsy shop is a reflection of your creativity and passion, so let it evolve with you.

As you embark on this journey, keep in mind that success doesn't come overnight. It takes time, effort, and persistence. But with dedication and a willingness to learn, you can turn your crafting hobby into a successful business. This book is here to guide you every step of the way, providing you with the knowledge and tools you need to thrive on Etsy.

Setting up your Etsy shop is a significant milestone, and it's the foundation upon which you'll build your business. By taking the time to do it right, you're setting yourself up for success. So take a deep breath, follow the steps outlined in this chapter, and get ready to share your creations with the world.

Sure! Here is the first section on "Crafting Your Brand Identity." Given the extensive length you requested, I'll provide a detailed and conversational approach for this section first, and then proceed with the section on "Essential Tools and Resources.

CRAFTING YOUR BRAND IDENTITY

Imagine you're walking through a bustling market, surrounded by stalls selling everything from fresh produce to handmade jewelry. As you wander, a particular stall catches your eye. It's not just the products that draw you in, but the overall vibe—the colors, the signage, the way everything is displayed. There's something about it that feels cohesive and inviting. This is the power of a strong brand identity, and it's what you need to create for your Etsy shop.

Crafting your brand identity is like setting the stage for your online presence. It's about more than just a logo or a color scheme; it's the entire experience you create for your customers. Your brand identity communicates who you are, what you stand for, and what makes your products unique. It's the story you tell through every element of your shop, from your photos to your product descriptions to your packaging.

Let's start with the basics. Your brand identity begins with your shop name. This is the first thing potential customers will see, so it needs to be memorable and reflective of your products and style. Spend some time brainstorming names that capture the essence of your brand. Think about words that describe your products, your creative process, and your values. Once you have a few ideas, test them out. Say them out loud, write them down, and see how they look. Remember, your shop name will be part of your web address, so make sure it's easy to spell and remember.

Next, consider your brand's visual elements. This includes your logo, color palette, fonts, and overall aesthetic. Your logo is a visual representation of your brand, so it should be unique and easily recognizable. If you're not a graphic designer, don't worry. There are plenty of online tools, like Canva, that offer easy-to-use templates to create a professional-looking logo. Your color palette should be consistent across all your branding materials, from your Etsy shop banner to your social

18

media profiles to your packaging. Choose colors that reflect your brand's personality and style. Are you bold and vibrant, or calm and soothing? Your fonts should also be consistent and easy to read. Stick to one or two fonts to keep things simple and cohesive.

Now that you have your visual elements in place, let's talk about your brand's voice. This is how you communicate with your customers through your product descriptions, social media posts, and any other written content. Your brand voice should reflect your personality and values. Are you friendly and approachable, or more formal and professional? Think about how you want your customers to feel when they read your content. Use language that resonates with them and feels authentic to you.

Your brand story is another crucial element of your identity. This is the narrative that explains who you are, why you started your shop, and what makes your products special. Your story should be woven into every aspect of your brand, from your "About" section to your social media posts to your product packaging. People love to know the story behind the products they buy, so don't be afraid to share your journey and what inspires you. Be genuine and let your passion shine through.

Consistency is key when it comes to building a strong brand identity. Every element of your shop should work together to create a cohesive experience for your customers. This means using the same colors, fonts, and tone of voice across all your branding materials. It also means being consistent in how you present your products. Your product photos should have a consistent style, whether that means using the same background, lighting, or props. This helps create a professional and polished look that builds trust with your customers.

Don't forget about your packaging. This is an often-overlooked aspect of branding, but it's an important part of the customer experience. Your packaging should reflect your brand's style and values, and it should make your customers feel excited to receive their order. Consider adding a personal touch, like a handwritten thank-you note or a small freebie. This not only enhances the unboxing experience but also helps build a connection with your customers.

Building a strong brand identity takes time and effort, but it's an investment that will pay off in the long run. A well-crafted brand sets you apart from the competition and creates a loyal customer base that will keep coming back for more. As you continue to grow and evolve your shop, don't be afraid to revisit and refine your brand identity. Stay true to your vision, but be open to making changes as needed to keep your brand fresh and relevant.

Let's move on to the next essential step in setting up your Etsy shop: gathering the tools and resources you'll need to succeed. From photography equipment to marketing tools, having the right resources at your disposal can make all the difference in building a successful online business.

ESSENTIAL TOOLS AND RESOURCES

Running a successful Etsy shop requires more than just creativity and passion. You'll need a variety of tools and resources to help you manage your business, create high-quality products, and reach your target audience. Let's dive into some of the essential tools and resources you'll need to get your shop up and running.

First and foremost, you'll need a reliable computer and internet connection. This might seem obvious, but it's the foundation of your online business. Whether you're managing your listings, communicating with customers, or promoting your shop on social media, you'll be spending a lot of time online. Make sure your computer is up to the task and that you have a stable internet connection to avoid any disruptions.

Next, let's talk about photography equipment. High-quality product photos are crucial for attracting customers and showcasing your products in the best light. You don't need to invest in expensive equipment right away, but having a good camera and some basic lighting equipment can make a big difference. A smartphone with a good camera can work, but if you want to take your photos to the next level, consider investing in a DSLR camera. Good lighting is essential for clear, bright photos. Natural light is great, but if you're shooting indoors, you might want to invest in some affordable lighting equipment like softbox lights or a ring light.

In addition to your camera and lighting, you'll need a few other photography accessories. A tripod can help keep your camera steady and ensure sharp photos. If you're shooting small products like jewelry, a lightbox can help create a clean, professional look. Backgrounds and props can also enhance your photos and help tell your brand story. Choose backgrounds that complement your products and reflect your brand's style.

Once you have your photos, you'll need some basic photo editing software to make any necessary adjustments. There are plenty of free options available, like GIMP or Canva, as well as more advanced paid options like Adobe Photoshop or Lightroom. Editing your photos can help enhance their quality and ensure they look their best.

In addition to photography equipment, there are a few other tools that can help you manage your shop more efficiently. An inventory management system can help you keep track of your products, materials, and supplies. This is especially important as your shop grows and you start to carry more products. There are plenty of software options available, from simple spreadsheets to more advanced inventory management systems like TradeGecko or Stitch Labs.

Shipping is another crucial aspect of running an Etsy shop, and having the right tools can make the process much smoother. A good postal scale is essential for accurately weighing your packages and calculating shipping costs. Shipping labels can save you time and hassle at the post office. You can print them at home using a regular printer or invest in a label printer for a more professional look. Etsy offers discounted shipping labels through their platform, so take advantage of this feature to save on shipping costs.

When it comes to packaging, having the right materials can make all the difference. Invest in sturdy boxes or mailers to protect your products during shipping. Bubble wrap, packing peanuts, or tissue paper can help keep your items safe and secure. Don't forget about the little details, like thank-you notes or branded stickers, that can enhance the unboxing experience and leave a lasting impression on your customers.

Marketing is another key aspect of running a successful Etsy shop, and there are plenty of tools available to help you reach your target audience. Social media is a powerful marketing tool, and having a presence on platforms like Instagram, Facebook, and Pinterest can help you connect with potential customers and promote your products. Tools like Hootsuite or Buffer can help you schedule and manage your social media posts, making it easier to maintain a consistent presence.

Email marketing is another effective way to reach your customers and keep them engaged with your brand. Tools like Mailchimp or ConvertKit can help you create and send professional-looking emails, manage your subscriber list, and track the performance of your campaigns. Consider offering an incentive, like a discount code, to encourage customers to sign up for your email list.

SEO, or search engine optimization, is crucial for getting your products found on Etsy. Using the right keywords in your titles, descriptions, and tags can help improve your search rankings and attract more customers. Tools like Marmalead or eRank can help you research and choose the best keywords for your listings. Etsy's built-in analytics can also provide valuable insights into how your listings are performing and where you can make improvements.

Finally, don't forget about the importance of staying organized and managing your time effectively. Running an Etsy shop involves juggling a lot of different tasks, from creating products to managing orders to promoting your shop. Tools like Trello or Asana can help you keep track of your tasks and stay organized. Setting aside specific times each day or week to work on your shop can also help you stay on track and avoid feeling overwhelmed.

Running an Etsy shop is a lot of work, but having the right tools and resources can make the process much smoother and more enjoyable. As you continue on your journey, remember that there's always more to learn and new tools to discover. Stay curious, stay organized, and most importantly,

CHAPTER 2: UNDERSTANDING YOUR MARKET

IDENTIFYING YOUR NICHE

Identifying your niche is like finding your unique voice in a world full of noise. It's about discovering what makes your products special and how they fit into the larger market. Think of it as carving out a space that's entirely your own, where your creativity and passion can shine brightly. This is a crucial step in building a successful Etsy shop, and it's one that requires thought, research, and a bit of soul-searching.

Imagine you're setting up a shop in a busy marketplace. There are hundreds of stalls, each selling something different. Some stalls are crowded with customers, while others are quiet and overlooked. The stalls that attract the most attention are often those that offer something unique, something that stands out. This is what you want for your Etsy shop—a niche that draws people in and keeps them coming back.

Finding your niche starts with understanding your own interests and strengths. What do you love to create? What are you passionate about? Your niche should be something that excites you, something that you can see yourself working on day after day. If you're not passionate about your niche, it will be hard to sustain your business in the long run. Think about the hobbies and interests that bring you joy. Maybe it's knitting, jewelry making, painting, or woodworking. Whatever it is, it should be something that you genuinely enjoy and are good at.

Once you've identified your passions, it's time to think about how they translate into products. What can you make that others will want to buy? This is where market research comes in. Start by looking at other sellers on Etsy. What are they offering? What seems to be popular? Pay attention to the details—the styles, the price points, the descriptions. This will give you a sense of what's already out there and help you identify gaps in the market.

Let's say you're passionate about knitting. You love creating cozy scarves and intricate sweaters. A quick search on Etsy reveals that there are thousands of knitted items for sale. This might feel discouraging at first, but don't worry. Instead of viewing this as competition, see it as an opportunity to find your unique angle. What can you offer that's different from everyone else? Maybe you specialize in eco-friendly yarns or create custom designs. Perhaps your pieces have a modern twist, or you offer a personalized service. Your niche is the unique combination of your skills, interests, and what the market needs.

Another key part of identifying your niche is understanding your target audience. Who are you creating for? Who do you want to reach with your products? Your target audience will influence everything from your product design to your marketing strategy. Start by thinking about the people who would appreciate your work. Are they young professionals, stay-at-home parents, fashion-forward teens, or retirees looking for a hobby? The more specific you can be, the better.

Let's go back to the knitting example. If you decide to focus on eco-friendly yarns, your target audience might be environmentally conscious consumers who are willing to pay a bit more for sustainable products. These customers might be interested in the story behind your materials, and they might appreciate knowing that their purchase supports ethical practices. Understanding your audience helps you tailor your products and messaging to their needs and interests.

Once you have a sense of your niche and target audience, it's time to test your ideas. Start by creating a few prototypes and getting feedback. Share your creations with friends and family, or post them on social media to see what kind of response you get. You might even consider doing a small test run on Etsy to gauge interest. Pay attention to the feedback you receive and be open to making adjustments. This is all part of the process of refining your niche.

It's also important to think about the practical aspects of your niche. Can you source the materials you need easily and affordably? Can you produce your products at a scale that

27

makes sense for your business? Are there any legal or regulatory considerations you need to be aware of? For example, if you're creating products for children, there might be specific safety standards you need to meet. Make sure you do your research and understand the requirements for your niche.

As you refine your niche, don't be afraid to let your personality shine through. Your unique perspective and style are what will set you apart from other sellers. Maybe you have a quirky sense of humor that you can incorporate into your product descriptions, or you're inspired by a specific cultural heritage that you can highlight in your designs. Whatever it is, let it be a part of your brand.

Identifying your niche is not a one-time process. It's something that evolves over time as you learn more about your customers and what they want. Stay curious and open to new ideas. Keep an eye on trends and be willing to adapt. Your niche might shift as you discover new interests or as the market changes. That's okay. The key is to stay true to yourself and your passions, while also being responsive to your customers' needs.

Let's imagine you've decided to focus on creating eco-friendly knitted items. You've identified your target audience as environmentally conscious consumers, and you've done your research to find sustainable materials. You've tested your products and received positive feedback. Now it's time to start building your brand around this niche.

Your brand is the face of your business, and it should reflect your niche in every way. From your shop name to your logo to your product descriptions, everything should communicate your commitment to sustainability. Use your "About" section to share your story and explain why eco-friendly practices are important to you. Highlight the unique features of your products and what sets them apart. Use keywords in your listings that will attract your target audience, such as "sustainable," "eco-friendly," and "handmade."

Promote your niche on social media and through other marketing channels. Share behind-the-scenes photos of your creative process, or write blog posts about the importance of sustainability in crafting. Engage with your audience and build a community around your brand. The more you can connect with your customers and show them the value of your niche, the more successful your shop will be.

In summary, identifying your niche is about finding the intersection of your passions, skills, and what the market needs. It's about understanding your target audience and creating products that speak to them. It's about building a brand that reflects your unique perspective and values. And most importantly, it's about staying true to yourself while being open to learning and evolving. Your niche is the foundation of your Etsy shop, and getting it right will set you up for long-term success.

Now that you've identified your niche, let's move on to the next step: creating products that your customers will love. In the next chapter, we'll dive into product development and how to create items that stand out in the crowded Etsy marketplace.

Understanding your market is like learning the rules of a game before you start playing. It's essential, especially when you're entering the vibrant, competitive world of Etsy. Think of it this way: you wouldn't walk into a chess tournament without knowing how to play chess. Similarly, you shouldn't dive into selling on Etsy without thoroughly understanding the marketplace, your competitors, and your unique position within it. In this chapter, we'll explore how to research your competitors and identify your Unique Selling Proposition (USP), two crucial steps that will lay the foundation for your success.

Let's start with researching your competitors. Imagine you're opening a new coffee shop. You wouldn't just throw open the doors and hope for the best. You'd scout the area, check out other coffee shops, and see what they're doing right—and wrong. The same principle applies when setting up your Etsy shop.

To begin, you need to identify who your competitors are. This can be a fascinating exercise, almost like a treasure hunt. Fire up your computer, go to Etsy, and type in keywords related to the products you plan to sell. If you're making handmade jewelry, type "handmade jewelry" into the search bar. If you're crafting personalized stationery, type "personalized stationery." The shops that appear on the first page of results are your primary competitors. These shops are doing well, and there's a lot you can learn from them.

As you browse through these shops, take note of their product offerings, pricing, and overall presentation. Notice the little details how they photograph their products, the words they use in their descriptions, and how they structure their listings. It's like being a detective, piecing together what makes these shops successful. This isn't about copying what they do but understanding the landscape and figuring out how you can position yourself uniquely.

Next, delve into the details of these top-performing shops. Spend some time exploring their listings. Read through their product descriptions carefully. Notice the keywords they use. Keywords are crucial because they help potential customers find products through search. Pay attention to how your competitors describe their items. Are they focusing on the materials used, the craftsmanship, the uniqueness of the design? All these details matter.

Photos are another critical aspect to consider. Etsy is a visual marketplace, and high-quality photos can make or break a sale. Look at the images your competitors are using. Are they well-lit? Do they show the product from multiple angles? Do they include lifestyle shots that show the product in use? Take notes on what you like and what you think could be improved. Visual presentation is a huge part of what makes a shop appealing to customers.

Pricing is another significant factor. Check out the prices your competitors are charging for similar items. Pricing can be tricky because you don't want to undervalue your work, but you also need to be competitive. Consider the cost of your materials, the time it takes to create your products, and your overhead costs. Look for patterns in how successful shops price their items and use that as a guideline. Remember, your pricing should reflect the value of your work and the market demand.

Customer reviews are a goldmine of information. They give you insight into what customers love and what they don't. Read through the reviews of your competitors' products. What do customers praise? What do they complain about? Look for common themes. If multiple customers mention that a product arrived beautifully packaged, take note. If there are consistent complaints about slow shipping times, that's also valuable information. Use this feedback to understand customer expectations and find ways to exceed them.

After gathering all this information, it's time to synthesize it. Look at your notes and identify the strengths and weaknesses of your competitors. What are they doing well? Where are they falling short? This analysis will help you see where there might be gaps in the market that you can fill. For example, if you notice that many shops offer beautiful handmade candles but none of them use eco-friendly packaging, that could be an opportunity for you to stand out.

FINDING YOUR UNIQUE SELLING PROPOSITION

Your USP is what sets you apart from everyone else. It's the reason customers should choose your products over others. Finding your USP requires a bit of soul-searching and a lot of creativity.

Start by thinking about what makes your products special. This could be anything from the materials you use to the story behind your brand. Are your products made from sustainably sourced materials? Do you have a unique design process? Is there a personal story that inspired your business? Customers on Etsy love to connect with the maker behind the products, so your personal story can be a powerful part of your USP.

Consider the benefits of your products. Features are important, but benefits are what really sell. Features are the tangible aspects of your products, like the fact that your candles are made from 100% soy wax. Benefits, on the other hand, are the positive outcomes your customers experience, like a cleaner burn and less soot. Focus on the benefits that make your products superior to others.

Think about your target audience. Who are they? What do they value? Understanding your audience is key to defining your USP. If you're targeting environmentally conscious consumers, your USP might focus on the sustainability of your products. If you're targeting busy professionals, your USP might highlight the convenience and efficiency of your products. Tailor your USP to resonate with your target audience's needs and values.

Your USP should also be reflected in every aspect of your shop. Your product descriptions should highlight your unique features and benefits. Your shop's "About" section should tell your story and emphasize what makes you different. Your photos should visually convey the quality and uniqueness of your products. Every element of your shop should work together to communicate your USP clearly and consistently.

To truly understand your market, it's important to keep an eye on trends. Trends can give you insights into what customers are looking for and how you can adapt your products to meet those needs. Follow industry blogs, social media, and even fashion magazines to stay updated on the latest trends. On Etsy, you can use the "Trending Now" section to see what's popular. Trends can be a great source of inspiration, but make sure to stay true to your brand and not just chase trends for the sake of it.

Building a successful Etsy shop is an ongoing process of learning and adapting. Regularly check in on your competitors, see what new trends are emerging, and listen to your customers' feedback. The more you know about your market, the better equipped you'll be to adapt and thrive. Pay attention to what works and what doesn't, and don't be afraid to make changes. Your Etsy shop is a reflection of your creativity and passion, so let it evolve with you.

One of the best ways to continuously understand your market is to engage with your customers. Ask for feedback, conduct surveys, and interact with them on social media. Their insights can provide valuable information on what they like and what they wish you would offer. Building a relationship with your customers not only helps you improve your products but also creates a loyal customer base.

Think of understanding your market as building a strong foundation for your business. Without this foundation, it's challenging to grow and sustain your shop. By thoroughly researching your competitors and clearly defining your USP, you're setting yourself up for success. You're not just another shop on Etsy; you're a brand with a unique story and products that people love.

As you embark on this journey, remember that success doesn't come overnight. It takes time, effort, and persistence. But with dedication and a willingness to learn, you can turn your crafting hobby into a successful business. This book is here to guide you every step of the way, providing you with the knowledge and tools you need to thrive on Etsy.

So, roll up your sleeves, put on your detective hat, and dive into the world of Etsy with curiosity and enthusiasm. The more you understand your market, the better prepared you'll be to create products that resonate with your customers and stand out in a crowded marketplace. Your journey to Etsy success starts with understanding your market, and with this knowledge, you'll be well on your way to turning your crafting dreams into reality.

Remember, your competitors aren't just your rivals; they're also your teachers. Learn from them, but also strive to carve out your own unique space. Your USP is what will make you memorable and keep customers coming back. Stay curious, stay inspired, and keep pushing forward. The world is waiting to see what you create.

CHAPTER 3: CREATING CRAFT PRODUCTS THAT SELL

Crafting products that resonate with buyers on Etsy and leveraging platforms like TikTok to amplify your reach can be a game-changer for anyone venturing into the world of online craft sales. This chapter is dedicated to helping you understand the nuances of product development and the art of crafting high-quality items that not only attract buyers but also encourage repeat purchases. By the end of this chapter, you'll have a solid foundation on how to create desirable products and maintain the quality that keeps customers coming back.

PRODUCT DEVELOPMENT TIPS

Embarking on the journey of product development is akin to setting off on an adventure. It's filled with discovery, creativity, and the occasional challenge. To ensure your products stand out in a crowded marketplace like Etsy, you need to blend originality with practicality, while also keeping your potential customers' preferences at the forefront.

First, start with what you know and love. Your passion will shine through in your products, making them more appealing to buyers. If you enjoy creating jewelry, delve deep into that niche. If knitting is your forte, let your needles dance to the rhythm of your creativity. The key is to start with something you're passionate about, as this will not only make the process enjoyable but also infuse your creations with a unique touch that sets them apart.

Market research is an invaluable tool in product development. Before you commit to a product line, spend time exploring what's currently trending on Etsy. Look at the bestsellers in your chosen category and analyze what makes them popular. Pay attention to product descriptions, pricing, and customer reviews. This research will give you insights into what customers are looking for and how you can position your products to meet those needs.

Another critical aspect of product development is identifying your target audience. Understanding who your customers are, their preferences, and their buying behaviors can help you tailor your products to meet their needs. Are you targeting young adults who love quirky, handmade jewelry, or are you aiming for a more mature audience that appreciates elegant, handcrafted home decor? Defining your target market will help you focus your efforts and create products that have a higher chance of selling.

Once you have a clear idea of what you want to create and who you're creating it for, the next step is to sketch out your ideas. This doesn't have to be a professional drawing; even a simple sketch can help you visualize your product and make any necessary adjustments before you start crafting. Think of it as a blueprint that guides you through the creation process.

Material selection is another crucial step in product development. The quality of your materials directly impacts the final product, so choose wisely. Invest in high-quality materials that not only look good but also stand the test of time. If you're making jewelry, consider using hypoallergenic metals and durable stones. For knitwear, opt for soft, breathable yarns that feel comfortable against the skin. Your materials should enhance the beauty and functionality of your products, making them desirable to customers.

Prototyping is an essential part of the product development process. Create a few samples of your product to test out different designs, materials, and techniques. This experimentation phase allows you to refine your product and ensure it meets your quality standards before you start mass production. Don't be afraid to make changes and try new approaches; this is the time to perfect your craft.

Pricing your products correctly is a critical aspect of product development. You need to strike a balance between covering your costs and making a profit while also keeping your prices competitive. Consider all the expenses involved in creating your product, including materials, labor, and overhead costs. Factor in a fair profit margin that compensates you for your time and effort. Research similar products on Etsy to get an idea of the going rates and ensure your prices are in line with market expectations.

Packaging is often overlooked in product development, but it plays a significant role in the overall customer experience. Attractive, eco-friendly packaging can enhance the perceived value of your product and leave a lasting impression on your customers. Invest in quality packaging materials and consider adding personal touches, such as handwritten notes or branded stickers, to make your customers feel special.

Finally, don't underestimate the power of feedback. Once you start selling your products, pay close attention to customer reviews and feedback. This information is invaluable for refining your products and improving your offerings. Don't be discouraged by negative feedback; instead, use it as an opportunity to learn and grow. Continuous improvement is key to long-term success on Etsy.

CRAFTING HIGH-QUALITY ITEMS

Creating high-quality items is at the heart of a successful Etsy shop. High-quality craftsmanship not only sets your products apart from mass-produced items but also builds trust with your customers, encouraging repeat business and positive word-of-mouth referrals.

The first step in crafting high-quality items is honing your skills. Regardless of your craft, investing time in learning and improving your techniques is essential. There are countless resources available, from online tutorials and workshops to community classes and craft fairs. Take advantage of these opportunities to learn new skills, discover innovative techniques, and stay updated on industry trends.

Attention to detail is a hallmark of high-quality craftsmanship. Whether you're knitting a scarf, painting a canvas, or sculpting clay, paying close attention to the small details can make a significant difference in the final product. This means taking the time to ensure your stitches are even, your brush strokes are smooth, and your clay is free of air bubbles. Customers notice and appreciate the effort you put into creating a flawless product.

Using high-quality materials is another key factor in crafting high-quality items. The materials you choose can significantly impact the durability, appearance, and overall quality of your products. Invest in the best materials you can afford, as this will not only enhance the quality of your products but also justify a higher price point. Remember, customers are willing to pay more for items that are made with superior materials and craftsmanship.

Consistency is crucial when it comes to maintaining high quality. Each item you create should meet the same high standards, ensuring your customers receive a product that matches their expectations every time. Establishing a consistent workflow and quality control process can help you achieve this. Create a checklist of quality criteria that each product must meet before it's shipped to a customer. This could include checking for loose threads, ensuring even painting or varnishing, and confirming that all components are securely attached.

One way to ensure consistent quality is to create templates or patterns for your products. This is especially useful if you're producing multiple items in the same style or design. Templates can help you maintain uniformity in size, shape, and overall appearance, making it easier to produce high-quality items consistently. They also streamline the production process, saving you time and reducing the risk of errors.

The finishing touches are what truly elevate a product from good to exceptional. Taking the time to add these final details can significantly enhance the quality and appeal of your items. This could include adding a professional finish to your jewelry, such as polishing or plating, or applying a protective varnish to your woodwork. These finishing touches not only improve the appearance of your products but also increase their durability, making them more attractive to customers.

Customer feedback is an invaluable tool for maintaining and improving the quality of your products. Encourage your customers to leave reviews and share their thoughts on your items. This feedback can provide valuable insights into what you're doing well and where there's room for improvement. Pay close attention to any recurring issues or suggestions and use this information to refine your products and processes. Showing your customers that you value their input and are committed to continuous improvement can also enhance your reputation and build customer loyalty.

Another important aspect of crafting high-quality items is taking care of your tools and equipment. Regular maintenance and proper storage of your tools can extend their lifespan and ensure they function correctly. Clean your tools after each use and store them in a dry, organized space. Sharp tools, such as scissors or knives, should be regularly sharpened to ensure clean cuts, and any machinery, such as sewing machines or pottery wheels, should be serviced according to the manufacturer's recommendations. Taking care of your tools ensures that they perform at their best, helping you produce high-quality items.

Investing in your workspace is also crucial for crafting high-quality items. A well-organized, clean, and comfortable workspace can significantly impact your productivity and the quality of your work. Ensure your workspace is well-lit and equipped with all the necessary tools and materials. Organize your supplies in a way that makes them easily accessible and keep your workspace clean to avoid any accidents or mishaps that could affect the quality of your products. A dedicated, inspiring workspace can also boost your creativity and motivation, helping you produce your best work.

As you grow your Etsy shop and your product range, consider collaborating with other artisans or hiring skilled assistants to help you maintain quality and meet demand. Collaborations can bring fresh perspectives and new techniques to your work, enhancing the quality and diversity of your products. Hiring assistants allows you to delegate tasks and focus on the aspects of crafting that you're most passionate about. Ensure that any collaborators or assistants are trained to meet your quality standards and share your commitment to craftsmanship.

Finally, remember that high-quality crafting is an ongoing journey. There will always be new skills to learn, techniques to master, and materials to explore. Embrace this journey with curiosity and a willingness to experiment and evolve. Continuously seek out opportunities for growth and improvement, whether through formal education, self-directed learning, or simply trying new things in your craft. This commitment to excellence will not only enhance the quality of your products but also keep your creative spirit alive and thriving.

Creating craft products that sell on Etsy is a blend of creativity, skill, and business acumen. By focusing on product development and high-quality craftsmanship, you can create items that stand out in a crowded marketplace and attract loyal customers. Remember, the key to success is to stay passionate about your craft, continuously strive for improvement, and always keep your customers' needs and preferences at the forefront of your mind. With dedication and hard work, you can turn your creative passion into a thriving business on Etsy.

PRICING STRATEGIES FOR MAXIMUM PROFIT

Crafting beautiful, high-quality items is just the beginning of your journey as an Etsy seller. The next crucial step is setting the right prices for your products. Pricing can make or break your business. Too high, and you might scare away potential buyers; too low, and you won't cover your costs, let alone make a profit. This chapter is dedicated to demystifying pricing strategies, helping you find that sweet spot where your products are competitively priced yet profitable.

Imagine you've spent countless hours perfecting your craft, and now your products are ready to hit the Etsy marketplace. But one lingering question remains—how much should you charge? Pricing is not just about covering your costs; it's about understanding your market, your value, and positioning your products in a way that appeals to your ideal customers while ensuring you make a profit.

Let's start by talking about the foundation of pricing knowing your costs. It's crucial to understand every penny that goes into creating your product. This includes the cost of materials, time, and overhead expenses. Think of your materials: the fabric for that handmade dress, the beads for that intricate necklace, or the type of paint for that custom artwork. Each element has a cost, and it's important to track these expenses meticulously. But materials are just one part of the equation.

Your time is arguably your most valuable asset. Whether you're knitting a scarf, sculpting clay, or painting a masterpiece, your time is precious. But how do you quantify it? One approach is to decide on an hourly rate for your labor. Ask yourself, how much is your time worth? This isn't just about the time you spend crafting. It also includes the hours you spend on research, development, marketing, and customer service. When you factor in your time, you start to see the true cost of your product.

Overhead costs are another critical component. These are the expenses that keep your business running, such as electricity, internet, and packaging materials. Even the rent for your workspace or the cost of maintaining your tools falls into this category. It's easy to overlook these costs, but they add up and should be reflected in your pricing.

Now that you have a handle on your costs, it's time to think about profit margins. Profit is what makes your business sustainable and rewarding. To determine your profit margin, decide how much profit you want to make on each item. This might be a fixed dollar amount or a percentage of the cost. A common approach is to mark up your cost by a certain percentage to arrive at your selling price. For example, if your total cost to make a product is $20, and you want a 50% profit margin, you would price the product at $30.

However, pricing isn't just about covering costs and making a profit; it's also about perception. How do you want your customers to perceive your brand? Are you offering luxury items, everyday essentials, or something in between? Your pricing should reflect the value you offer and the market you're targeting. If you position your products as high-end, your prices should convey that sense of exclusivity and quality. Conversely, if you're targeting budget-conscious shoppers, your pricing should reflect affordability while still covering your costs and allowing for profit.

Market research plays a pivotal role in setting your prices. Spend time browsing Etsy and other platforms to see what similar products are selling for. Look at bestsellers in your category and analyze their pricing strategies. This doesn't mean you should copy their prices, but it gives you a benchmark. Consider what makes your products unique. Do you offer superior quality, a distinctive style, or exceptional customer service? These unique selling points can justify higher prices.

Psychological pricing is another strategy worth exploring. This involves setting prices that appeal to customers on a psychological level. For example, pricing an item at $29.99 instead of $30 can make it seem more affordable, even though the difference is just one cent. Similarly, offering tiered pricing or bundle deals can encourage customers to buy more. For instance, selling three items for the price of two can increase your overall sales and make customers feel they're getting a deal.

Offering discounts and promotions can also be a powerful tool. Limited-time offers or seasonal sales can create a sense of urgency and boost your sales. However, it's important to use this strategy judiciously. Frequent discounts can devalue your brand and lead customers to wait for sales rather than buying at full price. Balance is key. Use discounts to reward loyal customers, clear out old stock, or attract new buyers, but ensure they align with your overall pricing strategy.

Another aspect to consider is the perceived value of your products. This is where branding and presentation come into play. High-quality photos, detailed product descriptions, and positive customer reviews can all enhance the perceived value of your products, allowing you to command higher prices. Packaging also plays a role. Beautiful, eco-friendly packaging can make your products feel more luxurious and worth the price.

Don't underestimate the power of storytelling in your pricing strategy. Share the story behind your products, your creative process, and the passion you put into your work. This connection can make customers more willing to pay a premium for items that they feel have a unique story or personal touch. It's about building a brand that customers connect with and are willing to invest in.

Shipping costs are another factor to consider. Free shipping can be a significant selling point, but it's essential to ensure that the cost is factored into your pricing. You can either absorb the shipping cost into the price of the item or set a minimum order value to qualify for free shipping. Clear, upfront communication about shipping costs and delivery times can enhance customer satisfaction and reduce cart abandonment.

International pricing can also be a complex but rewarding aspect of your strategy. If you're selling to customers around the world, consider the additional costs involved, such as international shipping, customs duties, and currency conversion. Pricing your products appropriately for different markets can help you expand your reach while maintaining profitability. Research the pricing expectations and market conditions in different regions to ensure your prices are competitive yet profitable.

As your business grows, you may need to revisit and adjust your pricing strategy. Inflation, changes in material costs, and shifts in the market can all impact your pricing. Regularly review your costs, profit margins, and market conditions to ensure your prices remain competitive and profitable. Don't be afraid to adjust your prices as needed. It's better to make small, regular adjustments than to wait until you're forced to make a significant change.

Communicating your prices effectively is also important. Be transparent about your pricing and any additional costs, such as shipping or taxes. Clearly explain the value and benefits of your products, and don't shy away from highlighting what sets them apart from the competition. Transparency builds trust with your customers and can lead to higher satisfaction and repeat business.

Customer feedback can provide valuable insights into your pricing strategy. Pay attention to what your customers say about your prices. Are they willing to pay more for certain features or benefits? Are there any consistent complaints about pricing? Use this feedback to fine-tune your strategy and better meet your customers' needs. Engaging with your customers and showing that you value their opinions can also strengthen your brand and foster loyalty.

Finally, remember that pricing is both an art and a science. It requires a balance of analytical thinking and creative intuition.

Stay flexible and open to experimenting with different strategies. What works for one product or market might not work for another. Continually learn, adapt, and refine your approach to find the pricing sweet spot that maximizes your profit and keeps

Pricing your products for maximum profit involves a multifaceted approach. By understanding your costs, researching the market, and considering psychological and perceived value factors, you can set prices that are both competitive and profitable. Regularly review and adjust your pricing strategy to stay ahead of market changes and continue to provide value to your customers. With the right pricing strategy, you can turn your passion for crafting into a thriving business on Etsy.

CHAPTER 4: OPTIMIZING YOUR ETSY LISTINGS

Welcome to the next vital step in building your successful Etsy business. Now that you've got a grasp on creating and pricing your products, it's time to delve into the art and science of optimizing your Etsy listings. This chapter focuses on crafting compelling titles and descriptions and understanding the importance of keywords and SEO. These elements are crucial because they significantly influence how potential buyers find your products and decide whether to make a purchase. Let's dive into the details of making your listings not just good, but irresistible.

CRAFTING COMPELLING TITLES AND DESCRIPTIONS

Imagine scrolling through pages of Etsy listings, each one vying for your attention. What makes you stop and click on a particular item? Often, it's the title and the description that catch your eye. These are your first opportunities to make an impression on potential buyers, so they need to be engaging, informative, and persuasive.

Think of your title as the headline of a news article. It needs to be catchy and informative, yet concise. The goal is to immediately communicate what your product is while enticing the reader to learn more. To achieve this, focus on the most important aspects of your product what it is, what makes it unique, and why someone should buy it. For example, instead of a simple "Handmade Necklace," consider something like "Elegant Handmade Beaded Necklace with Swarovski Crystals - Perfect for Weddings and Special Occasions." This title not only describes the product but also hints at its use and special features.

While crafting your titles, it's crucial to balance creativity with clarity. Avoid using overly complicated language or trying to be too clever. Your primary aim is to ensure that your potential buyers immediately understand what you're selling. Think about the keywords that someone might use when searching for your product. These keywords should naturally fit into your title, making it both SEO-friendly and appealing to human readers.

Next, let's talk about product descriptions. Your description is where you can really sell your product by providing detailed information that helps the buyer make an informed decision. Start by putting yourself in the buyer's shoes. What information would you need to feel confident about making a purchase? This could include details about the materials used, the size and dimensions, the crafting process, and any unique features or benefits.

Begin your description with a strong opening that captures attention. This might be a brief story about the inspiration behind the product or a compelling statement about its uniqueness. For instance, "Inspired by the tranquil beauty of the ocean, this handmade beaded necklace features shimmering Swarovski crystals that capture the light with every movement. Whether you're dressing up for a special occasion or adding a touch of elegance to your everyday wear, this necklace is sure to turn heads."

As you continue, break down the key features and benefits of your product. Use clear, concise language and avoid unnecessary jargon. If your product has practical uses, explain them in a way that highlights its versatility. For example, if you're selling a handmade tote bag, you might describe how it's perfect for everything from grocery shopping to beach trips, thanks to its durable materials and spacious design.

Incorporate sensory details where possible. Describing the texture, color, and feel of your product can help potential buyers imagine owning and using it. For example, "The necklace is made with smooth, cool beads that feel wonderful against the skin, and the crystals catch the light beautifully, adding a touch of sparkle to any outfit."

Transparency is key in your descriptions. Be honest about your product's features and potential limitations. If the color might vary slightly due to the handmade nature of the item, mention that. If the item requires special care, provide clear instructions. This builds trust with your customers and reduces the likelihood of returns due to unmet expectations.

End your description with a strong closing that encourages the buyer to take action. This could be a reminder of the product's unique features, a mention of limited stock, or an invitation to check out customer reviews. For example, "This elegant necklace is one of our bestsellers, and with limited quantities available, it's sure to sell out quickly. Don't miss your chance to own this stunning piece—order now and add a touch of luxury to your jewelry collection."

THE IMPORTANCE OF KEYWORDS AND SEO

Now, let's turn our attention to the importance of keywords and search engine optimization (SEO). Understanding how to effectively use keywords can dramatically increase the visibility of your listings on Etsy and even on broader search engines like Google. This, in turn, can drive more traffic to your shop and boost your sales.

Keywords are the words and phrases that potential buyers use to search for products. By strategically incorporating these keywords into your titles, descriptions, and tags, you increase the chances of your listings appearing in search results. The first step is to brainstorm a list of keywords that are relevant to your product. Think about the terms your ideal customer might use when searching for an item like yours. This could include broad terms like "handmade jewelry" as well as more specific phrases like "Swarovski crystal necklace" or "beaded wedding jewelry."

Once you have your list, it's time to do some research. Use tools like Etsy's search bar, Google Trends, and keyword planners to see which terms are popular and relevant to your product. Pay attention to the search volume and competition for each keyword. High-volume keywords are searched frequently, but they may also have a lot of competition. On the other hand, more specific, long-tail keywords might have less competition and can help you reach a more targeted audience.

When you've identified your primary and secondary keywords, start incorporating them into your titles, descriptions, and tags. Your primary keyword should appear in your title, ideally towards the beginning. For example, "Swarovski Crystal Necklace - Handmade Beaded Wedding Jewelry." This not only helps with SEO but also immediately communicates the main features of your product to potential buyers.

In your description, weave your keywords naturally into the text. Avoid keyword stuffing, which is the practice of overloading your content with keywords in a way that feels forced or unnatural. This can negatively impact the readability of your description and might even hurt your SEO ranking. Instead, focus on writing engaging, informative content that naturally includes your keywords. For instance, "This Swarovski crystal necklace is perfect for adding a touch of elegance to your wedding day. Each bead is carefully handmade, ensuring a unique and stunning piece of jewelry."

Tags are another important element of SEO on Etsy. Tags are essentially keywords or phrases that describe your product. Etsy allows you to use up to 13 tags per listing, so make the most of this opportunity. Use a mix of broad and specific keywords to increase your chances of being found. For example, you might use tags like "handmade necklace," "Swarovski crystal," "beaded jewelry," "wedding accessories," and "bridal necklace."

In addition to using keywords, optimizing your listings involves creating high-quality content that resonates with both search engines and human readers. Search engines look for content that is relevant, informative, and engaging. This means writing descriptions that provide real value to potential buyers, using clear and concise language, and avoiding spelling and grammatical errors.

Visual content is also a key component of SEO. High-quality photos and videos can improve your search ranking and make your listings more appealing to potential buyers. Make sure your photos are clear, well-lit, and show your product from multiple angles. Consider adding a video that showcases your product in use, as this can provide a more dynamic and engaging view.

Another important aspect of SEO is maintaining an active and updated shop. Regularly adding new listings, updating existing ones, and keeping your shop's policies and about sections current can positively impact your search ranking. This shows search engines that your shop is active and relevant, which can improve your visibility in search results.

Customer reviews also play a significant role in SEO. Positive reviews can boost your credibility and trustworthiness, which can lead to higher search rankings. Encourage your customers to leave reviews by providing excellent customer service and following up with them after their purchase. Responding to reviews, both positive and negative, can also show potential buyers that you value their feedback and are committed to improving your shop.

Monitoring and analyzing your SEO efforts is crucial for ongoing success. Use Etsy's shop analytics and other tools to track the performance of your listings. Pay attention to which keywords are driving traffic and sales, and adjust your strategy as needed. SEO is not a one-time task; it's an ongoing process that requires regular attention and refinement.

Optimizing your Etsy listings is a multifaceted approach that involves crafting compelling titles and descriptions and understanding the importance of keywords and SEO. By taking the time to carefully craft your listings and strategically use keywords, you can increase your visibility, attract more potential buyers, and ultimately drive more sales. With these strategies in place, you'll be well on your way to creating a successful Etsy shop that stands out in a crowded marketplace.

USING HIGH-QUALITY IMAGES AND VIDEOS

Imagine stepping into a beautifully curated boutique, where each item is displayed with careful attention to lighting, angles, and presentation. That's the kind of experience you want to replicate for your customers online. High-quality images and videos are your virtual storefront, inviting shoppers to explore and appreciate your products. Let's delve into the details of creating compelling visuals that do justice to your craftsmanship.

When a potential buyer stumbles upon your Etsy listing, the first thing they see is the thumbnail image. This tiny preview is your chance to grab their attention and entice them to click through to your product page. It's akin to the cover of a book or the sign outside a store—it needs to be both eye-catching and informative. To achieve this, choose an image that clearly shows the main features of your product. Ensure it's well-lit, in focus, and framed to highlight the item's best attributes.

Lighting is one of the most critical elements of photography. Natural light is often the best option, as it provides a soft, flattering glow that enhances the colors and textures of your products. Set up near a window during the daytime, and avoid harsh, direct sunlight that can create unwanted shadows and glare. If natural light isn't available, invest in softbox lights or ring lights to create a similar effect. The goal is to achieve even, diffused lighting that makes your products look their best.

Consider the background as well. A clean, uncluttered background keeps the focus on your product. Neutral colors like white, gray, or light wood are often effective, as they don't distract from the item itself. However, don't be afraid to get creative if it suits your brand—just ensure the background complements rather than competes with your product. For instance, a rustic wooden board might be perfect for showcasing handmade pottery, while a bright, colorful backdrop could work well for playful, whimsical items.

Angles and composition are equally important. Show your product from multiple angles to give potential buyers a complete view. Include close-up shots to highlight intricate details, textures, and craftsmanship. Think about how the product is used or worn and incorporate those angles as well. For example, if you're selling a necklace, include images of it being worn to show its size and how it sits. This helps buyers visualize the product in real life, which can increase their confidence in making a purchase.

Staging can enhance the appeal of your product images. Props can add context and tell a story about how your product fits into a buyer's life. However, use props sparingly to ensure they don't overshadow the main item. For instance, if you're selling a coffee mug, you might include a cozy setup with a book and a blanket in the background to evoke a sense of warmth and comfort. The key is to enhance the visual appeal without cluttering the image.

Editing is the final step in creating high-quality images. Basic adjustments to brightness, contrast, and color balance can make a significant difference. There are many user-friendly editing tools available, from smartphone apps to professional software like Adobe Photoshop. The goal is to enhance your images while keeping them realistic and true to life. Over-editing can create an artificial look that may mislead buyers and lead to disappointment when they receive the actual product.

Now, let's talk about the power of video. While photos capture a single moment, videos can provide a dynamic, multi-dimensional view of your products. A well-produced video can bring your listings to life, showcasing how your items look, move, and function in real time. This is particularly useful for products that have moving parts, unique features, or require a demonstration.

Start with a clear plan for your video. What do you want to highlight? What story do you want to tell? A good video doesn't have to be long; even a 30-second clip can be effective if it's focused and well-executed. Use a tripod or stabilizer to keep your camera steady, and ensure your lighting is consistent with your photos. Natural light works well for videos too, but you might need additional lighting to ensure every detail is visible.

Begin your video with a wide shot that shows the entire product. This gives viewers an overall sense of the item. Then, move to close-up shots to highlight important details and features. If your product has any special functions, demonstrate them clearly. For example, if you're selling a handmade journal, show the quality of the paper, the binding, and how it opens and closes. This helps viewers understand what sets your product apart and builds their confidence in its quality.

Adding narration or background music can enhance your video. Narration allows you to explain features and benefits while showing them, making the video both informative and engaging. Background music can set the mood and make the video more enjoyable to watch, but choose music that complements your brand and doesn't distract from the product. There are many royalty-free music options available online.

Editing your video is crucial to create a polished final product. Trim any unnecessary footage, and make sure the transitions between shots are smooth. Basic editing tools like iMovie or Adobe Premiere Rush can help you create professional-looking videos without a steep learning curve. Add captions or text overlays to highlight key features or provide additional information, but keep them concise and easy to read.

Once you've created your images and videos, it's time to upload them to your Etsy listings. Etsy allows you to add up to ten photos and one video per listing, so make the most of this opportunity. Use a variety of images to show different angles and features, and include your video to provide an engaging, dynamic view. The first image you upload becomes the thumbnail, so choose the one that best represents your product and grabs attention.

High-quality visuals can also enhance your social media presence. Platforms like Instagram are highly visual, and attractive images and videos can drive traffic to your Etsy shop. Use your best photos and videos to create engaging posts and stories that showcase your products. Tag your posts with relevant hashtags and include a link to your Etsy shop to make it easy for followers to find and buy your products.

Engaging with your audience on social media can also provide valuable feedback and insights. Pay attention to which images and videos get the most likes, comments, and shares. This can give you an idea of what resonates with your audience and guide you in creating future content. Responding to comments and messages builds a sense of community and can foster customer loyalty.

In conclusion, using high-quality images and videos is a powerful way to optimize your Etsy listings and attract more buyers. By paying attention to lighting, composition, and editing, you can create visuals that showcase your products in the best possible light. Videos add a dynamic element that can bring your products to life and provide valuable information to potential buyers. Together, these elements create a compelling visual experience that can drive traffic, increase sales, and help you build a successful Etsy shop. With a little effort and creativity, you can turn your visual content into one of your strongest selling tools.

Chapter 5: Mastering Etsy Shop Management

Welcome to the heart of your Etsy business, the management of your shop. Crafting beautiful products and optimizing your listings are critical, but maintaining an organized and efficient shop is equally important. Effective shop management ensures that orders are processed smoothly, inventory is well-maintained, and customers receive exceptional service. This chapter will delve into the nitty-gritty of managing orders and inventory and provide insights into delivering top-notch customer service.

MANAGING ORDERS AND INVENTORY

Imagine your Etsy shop as a bustling little boutique. Orders are flowing in, and your inventory is flying off the virtual shelves. To keep up with this demand, you need a streamlined system for managing orders and maintaining your inventory. It's the backbone of your business operations, ensuring that your products are available when customers want them and that orders are fulfilled promptly.

Start by establishing a reliable method for tracking your inventory. Whether you prefer digital tools or a good old-fashioned spreadsheet, the key is to keep it updated and accurate. List every product you have, including variations in color, size, or design. Each time you make a sale, update your inventory to reflect the change. This helps prevent overselling and ensures you can fulfill orders without delay.

An effective inventory system can save you time and reduce stress. Imagine how reassuring it is to know exactly how many pieces of each item you have at any given time. You won't have to scramble to check your stock or worry about disappointing a customer because you've run out of a popular item. Keeping your inventory organized also makes it easier to identify which products are your bestsellers and which ones might need a little extra promotion.

To streamline your inventory management, consider using inventory management software. These tools can sync with your Etsy shop, automatically updating your stock levels as sales come in. They can also help you analyze sales trends, forecast demand, and set reorder points to ensure you never run out of key items. Some popular options include QuickBooks Commerce, Craftybase, and TradeGecko.

Managing orders efficiently is equally important. When an order comes in, it's not just about packing and shipping the item. There's a process to follow to ensure everything goes smoothly. Start by setting up a system to handle orders as soon as they arrive. This could be a digital system where you track the status of each order—from received to fulfilled—or a physical system with folders or trays for different stages of the process.

The first step is to confirm the order. This is usually done automatically through Etsy, but it's good practice to review each order to ensure there are no special instructions or custom requests from the customer. If there are, make sure these are noted and followed through. Accurate and clear communication at this stage can prevent misunderstandings and mistakes.

Next, prepare the item for shipping. Carefully package your products to ensure they arrive in perfect condition. Use appropriate packing materials to protect your items during transit. For delicate items, consider using bubble wrap, packing peanuts, or foam inserts. For larger items, sturdy boxes and proper padding are essential. Always include a packing slip with the order details and a personal thank-you note to show your appreciation.

Shipping is a critical aspect of order management. Choose reliable shipping carriers and understand their delivery times and costs. Offering multiple shipping options, such as standard, expedited, and international shipping, can cater to different customer needs. Make sure to provide tracking information to your customers so they can monitor their order's progress. This not only builds trust but also reduces the likelihood of shipping-related inquiries.

Automation can be a game-changer in managing orders and inventory. Etsy offers integrations with various shipping and inventory management tools that can help automate many of these tasks. For example, tools like ShipStation or Pirate Ship can simplify the shipping process by printing labels, calculating postage, and sending tracking information to customers automatically. These tools save you time and reduce the potential for errors.

Handling returns and exchanges is another important aspect of order management. Set clear policies for returns and exchanges, and make sure these are communicated to your customers through your shop's policies page. Be prompt and courteous in handling return requests. While returns can be a hassle, a smooth and positive return experience can turn a dissatisfied customer into a loyal one.

Inventory management also involves planning for busy periods and sales events. The holiday season, for instance, can see a significant increase in orders. Plan ahead by stocking up on your bestsellers and ensuring you have enough packaging materials. Consider hiring temporary help if needed to keep up with the increased demand. Promotional events like Black Friday or Etsy's site-wide sales can also drive a surge in orders. Be prepared to manage these peaks without compromising on service quality.

Regularly reviewing your inventory and sales data is crucial for effective management. Analyze which products are selling well and which aren't. This can inform your decisions on what to produce more of and what to discontinue. Look at your profit margins and adjust your pricing or sourcing strategies if needed. Staying on top of your data helps you make informed decisions and keep your business profitable.

CUSTOMER SERVICE EXCELLENCE

Now, let's turn our attention to customer service, a cornerstone of any successful business. Excellent customer service goes beyond merely responding to inquiries; it's about creating a positive, memorable experience for your customers at every touchpoint. When customers feel valued and cared for, they are more likely to return and recommend your shop to others.

Start by setting the tone with clear, friendly communication. From the moment a customer visits your shop, they should feel welcomed and appreciated. Write a warm and engaging shop announcement that introduces yourself and your brand. Use the About section to share your story, your passion for crafting, and what makes your products special. This personal touch helps build a connection with potential buyers.

Respond to customer inquiries promptly and courteously. Whether a customer has a question about a product, shipping times, or a return, timely responses show that you value their business. Aim to respond within 24 hours, even if it's just to acknowledge their message and let them know you're working on a more detailed reply. Quick and helpful communication can make a big difference in customer satisfaction.

Going above and beyond in your interactions can turn a one-time buyer into a loyal customer. Personalize your communication whenever possible. Address customers by their names, reference their specific orders, and show genuine interest in their needs and preferences. For example, if a customer mentions they're buying a gift, ask if they'd like a special note included. These small gestures make customers feel special and appreciated.

Clear and detailed product descriptions also play a crucial role in customer service. By providing all the necessary information upfront, you can reduce the likelihood of customer inquiries and returns. Include details about the size, materials, care instructions, and any variations in color or design. Use high-quality photos that show the product from multiple angles, so customers know exactly what to expect.

Handling complaints and issues with grace is another key aspect of excellent customer service. Mistakes happen, and how you handle them can make all the difference. If a customer receives a damaged item or their order is delayed, apologize sincerely and offer a solution, whether it's a replacement, a refund, or a discount on their next purchase. Resolving issues quickly and fairly can turn a negative experience into a positive one.

Encouraging customer feedback and reviews is essential for building trust and improving your shop. After a purchase, follow up with a thank-you message and invite customers to leave a review. Positive reviews not only boost your shop's credibility but also provide valuable insights into what customers love about your products. Pay attention to any constructive criticism and use it to improve your offerings and service.

Building a community around your shop can enhance customer loyalty. Engage with your customers on social media, share behind-the-scenes content, and involve them in your creative process. Hosting giveaways, sharing user-generated content, and asking for their input on new designs are great ways to foster a sense of community and keep your customers engaged.

Offering exceptional customer service also means making your shop policies clear and fair. Outline your policies on shipping, returns, and exchanges in a way that's easy to understand. Transparency builds trust and sets clear expectations for your customers. If any issues arise, having well-defined policies can help resolve them smoothly.

Finally, always strive to improve your customer service. Regularly review your interactions with customers and look for areas where you can do better. Invest in training or resources that can help you enhance your communication skills and customer service strategies. Remember, happy customers are the best advertisement for your shop—they're more likely to return, leave positive reviews, and recommend your shop to others.

In conclusion, mastering Etsy shop management involves efficient order and inventory management combined with excellent customer service. By keeping your inventory organized, streamlining your order process, and providing exceptional service, you create a positive experience that encourages repeat business and fosters customer loyalty. With these strategies in place, you're well on your way to building a successful and thriving Etsy shop.

Handling Returns

Imagine you've just received a notification that a customer wants to return an item. It's natural to feel a mix of emotions—disappointment that the customer wasn't completely satisfied, concern about the impact on your business, and perhaps a bit of frustration over the added work. However, it's important to approach returns with a calm, professional demeanor. How you handle returns can significantly impact your customer's perception of your shop.

Start by establishing clear return policies. Make sure these policies are easy to find and understand on your Etsy shop page. A well-crafted return policy sets the expectations for both you and the customer. It should outline the conditions under which returns are accepted, the timeframe in which a return must be initiated, and who is responsible for the return shipping costs. Being upfront about your return policy helps prevent misunderstandings and provides a reference point when dealing with returns.

When a return request comes in, respond promptly. Acknowledge the customer's request and thank them for reaching out. Prompt communication shows that you value their business and are committed to resolving any issues. Even if the situation is not ideal, a courteous and professional response can go a long way in maintaining a positive relationship with the customer.

Next, understand the reason for the return. Is the item damaged? Did it not meet the customer's expectations? Was there a mistake in the order? Understanding the reason behind the return can help you address the issue effectively and prevent similar problems in the future. For instance, if an item was damaged during shipping, you might need to reassess your packaging methods. If a customer felt the item didn't match the description, you might need to improve your product photos or descriptions.

Once you understand the reason for the return, provide clear instructions for how the customer should proceed. If the item needs to be shipped back, provide details on how to package it securely and which shipping method to use. If you're covering the return shipping cost, send the customer a prepaid shipping label. Make the process as smooth and hassle-free as possible for the customer. This not only helps resolve the issue quickly but also demonstrates your commitment to customer satisfaction.

Processing the return efficiently is crucial. Once you receive the returned item, inspect it to ensure it meets the conditions outlined in your return policy. If the item is in good condition, promptly issue a refund or replacement as agreed upon with the customer. If there are any issues with the returned item, communicate these to the customer and work together to find a fair resolution. Keeping the customer informed throughout the process helps build trust and reduces any anxiety they might have about the return.

Offering a replacement instead of a refund can sometimes be a better option for both you and the customer. If the customer is open to it, a replacement allows you to retain the sale and the customer gets the product they wanted. This is particularly useful if the original item was damaged or had a defect. Make sure to expedite the replacement to show the customer that you're prioritizing their satisfaction.

Handling returns gracefully can turn a potentially negative experience into a positive one. When customers see that you're willing to go the extra mile to ensure their satisfaction, they're more likely to give your shop another chance. They might even leave a positive review or recommend your shop to others despite the initial issue. Remember, the goal is not just to resolve the return but to enhance the customer's overall experience with your shop.

HANDLING COMPLAINTS

Now, let's shift our focus to handling complaints. Complaints can be particularly challenging because they often come with a sense of urgency and emotion. However, they also provide valuable opportunities to improve your business and build stronger customer relationships.
When a complaint comes in, the first step is to listen. Take the time to read or listen to the customer's concerns thoroughly before responding. Customers want to feel heard and understood. By giving them your full attention, you're

showing respect and empathy, which can help defuse their frustration. Avoid interrupting or jumping to conclusions. Sometimes, just the act of listening can start to resolve the issue.

Respond to the complaint promptly. Quick responses show that you take the customer's concerns seriously. Even if you don't have a solution right away, acknowledge their message and let them know you're looking into it. This helps manage their expectations and shows that you're proactive in addressing their issue.

Empathy is key when handling complaints. Put yourself in the customer's shoes and imagine how you would feel in their situation. Respond with empathy and understanding, acknowledging their frustration or disappointment. Phrases like "I'm sorry to hear that you're unhappy with your purchase" or "I understand how frustrating this must be" can go a long way in calming the customer and building rapport.

After acknowledging the complaint, offer a solution. Depending on the nature of the complaint, this could be a refund, a replacement, or a discount on a future purchase. Be fair and reasonable in your offer, considering both the customer's experience and your business's sustainability. Sometimes, offering a little extra, like a small freebie or a handwritten apology note, can make a big difference in how the customer perceives the resolution.

Clear communication is crucial throughout the process. Keep the customer informed about what steps you're taking to resolve their issue and when they can expect a resolution. Transparency builds trust and reassures the customer that their concerns are being taken seriously. If there are any delays or complications, let them know immediately and explain why.

Sometimes, complaints can be an opportunity for learning and growth. Reflect on the feedback and consider whether there are any changes you can make to prevent similar issues in the future. For example, if multiple customers have complained about the same issue, it might be a sign that you need to improve your product descriptions, packaging, or quality control processes. Use complaints as a tool for continuous improvement.

It's also important to handle complaints professionally, even if they seem unreasonable or unfair. Stay calm and composed, and avoid responding defensively. Remember that your goal is to resolve the issue in a way that leaves the customer feeling satisfied. Sometimes, a difficult customer can be turned into a loyal one simply through excellent service and a positive resolution.

Negative reviews are another form of complaint that requires careful handling. While it's impossible to avoid negative reviews entirely, how you respond to them can impact your shop's reputation. When responding to a negative review, acknowledge the customer's experience and offer a resolution. Keep your response polite and professional, and avoid getting into public arguments. This shows potential customers that you're committed to customer satisfaction, even when things go wrong.

Encourage positive reviews by providing excellent service and follow-up. After resolving a complaint, politely ask the customer if they would consider updating their review to reflect the resolution. Many customers are willing to do this if they feel that their issue was handled well. Positive reviews can help offset the impact of negative ones and build a stronger reputation for your shop.

Handling returns and complaints effectively is an essential part of mastering Etsy shop management. By establishing clear return policies, responding promptly and empathetically to complaints, and using feedback to improve your business, you can turn potentially negative experiences into positive ones. This not only enhances customer satisfaction but also builds trust and loyalty, helping your shop thrive in the competitive world of Etsy.

CHAPTER 6: INTRODUCTION TO TIKTOK FOR BUSINESS

Welcome to a new chapter in your journey to mastering online sales harnessing the power of TikTok to drive traffic and sales to your Etsy shop. TikTok has exploded onto the social media scene with its short, engaging videos, and it offers a unique opportunity for businesses to reach a broad audience. This chapter will guide you through setting up your TikTok profile and navigating the platform's interface, helping you create a compelling presence that captures the interest of potential customers.

SETTING UP YOUR TIK TOK PROFILE

Imagine TikTok as a vast, bustling marketplace. Your profile is like your storefront, the first thing potential customers see. Setting it up correctly is crucial to making a great first impression and attracting followers who will become loyal customers.

The first step is to download the TikTok app and create an account. You can sign up using your email, phone number, or through a linked social media account. Choose the method that's most convenient for you. Once you're in, it's time to set up your profile.

Start with your username. This is your unique identity on TikTok, so choose something that reflects your brand. If possible, use the same name as your Etsy shop to maintain consistency across platforms. This makes it easier for customers to find and recognize you. If your preferred username is taken, try adding a creative twist, like including your niche or a keyword related to your products.

Next, move on to your profile picture. This small image is a powerful branding tool. Use your logo if you have one, or a high-quality image that represents your brand. The profile picture should be clear and easily recognizable, even when viewed as a small thumbnail. Think of it as your business card—it should be professional and instantly convey who you are.

Your bio is your chance to introduce yourself and your business. You have a limited number of characters, so make every word count. Start with a brief statement about what you offer. Highlight your unique selling points and what makes your products special. For example, if you sell handmade jewelry, you might write, "Handcrafted jewelry inspired by nature's beauty. Unique designs made with love." This not only tells visitors what you do but also adds a personal touch.

Include a call to action in your bio. Encourage visitors to check out your Etsy shop, follow you for updates, or visit your website. For example, "Shop our latest collection on Etsy! Link below." TikTok allows you to add a clickable link to your profile, so make sure to include a direct link to your

Etsy shop. This makes it easy for followers to browse your products and make a purchase.

Now that your profile is set up, let's dive into the heart of TikTok creating content. The beauty of TikTok is its simplicity. You don't need a professional studio or expensive equipment. All you need is your smartphone and a bit of creativity. Start by exploring the platform and getting a feel for the types of content that resonate with your audience. Look at what similar businesses are doing and take note of popular trends and challenges.

When you're ready to create your first video, tap the plus sign at the bottom of the screen. This opens the camera, where you can record a video up to 60 seconds long. You can also upload pre-recorded videos from your device. The recording interface is user-friendly, with options to add music, effects, and text. Experiment with different features to see what works best for your content.

Music is a key element of TikTok videos. The platform offers a vast library of songs and sound effects that you can use to enhance your videos. Choose music that fits the mood and theme of your content. Popular songs can help your videos gain traction, as users often search for videos featuring their favorite tracks. However, make sure the music doesn't overshadow your message—your products should always be the star of the show.

Adding text to your videos can help convey important information or emphasize key points. Use clear, readable fonts and keep the text brief. You can also use text to include calls to action, like "Check out our Etsy shop!" or "Follow us for more handmade creations." Text overlays are a great way to guide viewers and make your videos more engaging.

Editing your videos is where the magic happens. TikTok's editing tools are powerful and intuitive, allowing you to trim clips, add transitions, and apply filters. Take your time to polish your videos and make them as engaging as possible. Remember, the goal is to capture your audience's attention within the first few seconds and keep them watching until the end.

Once your video is ready, it's time to add captions and hashtags. Captions provide context and can help boost engagement. Write a brief, catchy caption that complements your video. Hashtags are essential for visibility. Use relevant hashtags to reach a broader audience. Mix popular hashtags with niche-specific ones to maximize your reach. For example, if you're showcasing a new jewelry piece, you might use #handmade jewelry, #EtsySeller, and #JewelryLovers.

After posting your video, engage with your audience. Respond to comments, like and share other users' content, and participate in trends and challenges. Building a community on TikTok requires active engagement. The more you interact with your followers, the more likely they are to support your business.

TikTok's analytics tools provide valuable insights into your content's performance. Use these tools to track metrics like views, likes, shares, and follower growth. Analyze which types of content perform best and adjust your strategy accordingly. Understanding your audience and their preferences can help you create more effective and engaging videos.

Consistency is key to building a strong presence on TikTok. Post regularly to keep your audience engaged and attract new followers. Develop a content calendar to plan your videos in advance. This helps ensure you always have fresh content to share and can take advantage of seasonal trends and events.

Collaborating with other TikTok creators can also boost your visibility. Find creators who share a similar audience and propose a collaboration. This could be a joint video, a shoutout, or a giveaway. Collaborations can introduce your shop to a wider audience and provide fresh content for your profile.

Paid advertising on TikTok is another way to reach a larger audience. TikTok offers various ad formats, including in-feed ads, branded hashtags, and sponsored effects. Consider running ads to promote special sales, new product launches, or to drive traffic to your Etsy shop. Paid ads can be a powerful tool when used strategically, helping you reach potential customers who might not find you organically.

Finally, remember to have fun with your TikTok content. The platform thrives on creativity and authenticity. Don't be afraid to show the personality behind your brand. Share behind-the-scenes glimpses of your creative process, introduce your team, or simply share what inspires you. Authentic content resonates with viewers and can help build a genuine connection with your audience.

NAVIGATING TIKTOK'S INTERFACE

Navigating TikTok's interface might seem overwhelming at first, but it's designed to be intuitive and user-friendly. Let's break down the main features and how to use them effectively for your business.

When you first open the TikTok app, you'll land on the "For You" page. This is the heart of TikTok, where the algorithm serves up a continuous stream of videos tailored to your interests. As you scroll through, you'll see content from a mix of popular creators and less-known users, based on what TikTok thinks you'll enjoy. This page is a great source of inspiration and trends, helping you understand what kind of content is currently popular.

To the right of the "For You" tab, you'll find the "Following" tab. Here, you'll see content exclusively from the users you follow. This is a more curated feed, filled with videos from creators you've chosen to keep up with. Engaging with content in this feed helps build relationships within the TikTok community.

At the bottom of the screen, you'll see five icons:

1. Home: Takes you back to the "For You" page.

2. Discover: This is where you can explore trending hashtags, sounds, and effects. It's an excellent place to find inspiration and discover popular content that you can adapt for your brand.

3. Create: Represented by a plus sign, this icon opens the camera to create a new video. We'll dive deeper into this shortly.

4. Inbox: This is where you'll find your notifications. This includes likes, comments, new followers, mentions, and messages. Keeping up with your notifications helps you stay engaged with your audience.

5. Profile: This icon takes you to your profile page, where you can view your own videos, see your followers and following lists, and edit your profile.

When you tap the **Create** button, you'll open the camera interface. Here's where the fun begins. The camera screen has several features to enhance your videos:

- **Flip:** This switches between the front and rear cameras.
- **Speed:** Allows you to record in slow motion or fast forward.

- **Beauty:** This feature smooths skin and enhances facial features.
- **Filters:** Choose from a variety of color filters to set the mood for your video.
- **Timer:** Set a countdown to start recording automatically after a few seconds.
- **Flash:** Turn the flash on or off.

At the top of the screen, you'll find options to add music and sounds. TikTok's extensive library includes popular songs, sound effects, and trending audio clips. Music is a key component of TikTok videos, so take some time to explore and find tracks that complement your content.

The recording button in the center allows you to start and stop recording. You can record multiple clips in a single video by pressing the button, stopping, and then pressing it again to continue recording. This is useful for creating dynamic, multi-scene videos.

On the right side, you'll see options to upload pre-recorded videos, add text, and use special effects. The effects library includes a wide range of options, from augmented reality (AR) effects to transitions and filters. Experiment with different effects to see what enhances your content.

Once you've recorded your video, tap the checkmark to move to the editing screen. Here, you can trim your clips, adjust the volume, add more effects, and insert text. TikTok's editing tools are robust yet easy to use, allowing you to polish your video and make it as engaging as possible.

After editing, you'll move to the posting screen. This is where you add your caption, hashtags, and tags. Captions should be short and catchy, providing context or adding humor to your video. Hashtags are crucial for visibility. Use a mix of popular and niche hashtags to reach a broader audience. TikTok also allows you to tag other users, which can help increase engagement and reach.

Before posting, you can choose who can view your video (everyone, friends, or just you) and whether to allow comments, duets, and stitches. Duets and stitches are unique TikTok features that allow other users to interact with your video. Duets let them record a video alongside yours, while stitches let them incorporate a clip from your video into their own. Enabling these features can increase your reach and engagement.

Once you've set everything up, hit "Post" to share your video with the world. Your video will appear on your profile and in the feeds of your followers. If you've used popular hashtags or sounds, it might also appear on the For You pages of other users, increasing its potential reach.

Navigating TikTok's interface effectively can help you create content that stands out and engages your audience. The platform's user-friendly design and powerful tools make it easy to produce high-quality videos, even if you're new to video creation. Spend some time exploring and experimenting with the different features to find what works best for your brand.

Engagement is key on TikTok. The more you interact with your audience, the more likely they are to engage with your content. Respond to comments, participate in challenges, and collaborate with other creators. Building a community around your brand can help you attract loyal followers and drive traffic to your Etsy shop.

TikTok's analytics tools provide valuable insights into your content's performance. Use these tools to track metrics like views, likes, shares, and follower growth. Analyze which types of content perform best and adjust your strategy accordingly. Understanding your audience and their preferences can help you create more effective and engaging videos.

Consistency is crucial for building a strong presence on TikTok. Develop a content calendar to plan your videos in advance and ensure you're posting regularly. This helps keep your audience engaged and attracts new followers. Keep an eye on trends and adapt them to your brand. Participating in trending challenges and using popular sounds can increase your visibility and help you reach a broader audience.

Collaborating with other TikTok creators can also boost your visibility. Find creators who share a similar audience and propose a collaboration. This could be a joint video, a shoutout, or a giveaway. Collaborations can introduce your shop to a wider audience and provide fresh content for your profile.

Paid advertising on TikTok is another way to reach a larger audience. TikTok offers various ad formats, including in-feed ads, branded hashtags, and sponsored effects. Consider running ads to promote special sales, new product launches, or to drive traffic to your Etsy shop. Paid ads can be a powerful tool when used strategically, helping you reach potential customers who might not find you organically.

Finally, remember to have fun with your TikTok content. The platform thrives on creativity and authenticity. Don't be afraid to show the personality behind your brand. Share behind-the-scenes glimpses of your creative process, introduce your team, or simply share what inspires you. Authentic content resonates with viewers and can help build a genuine connection with your audience.

Setting up your TikTok profile and navigating its interface are crucial steps in leveraging this powerful platform for your business. By creating engaging content, interacting with your audience, and staying on top of trends, you can build a strong presence on TikTok that drives traffic and sales to your Etsy shop. With a bit of creativity and consistency, TikTok can become a valuable tool in your marketing arsenal, helping you reach a broader audience and grow your business.

CHAPTER 7: INTRODUCTION TO TIKTOK FOR BUSINESS

TikTok has taken the world by storm with its engaging and often addictive short videos. For businesses, especially those running Etsy shops, TikTok offers a unique opportunity to reach a vast and diverse audience. But to harness the power of TikTok effectively, it's crucial to understand its algorithm. The algorithm is what determines which videos appear on users' "For You" page, making it the key to gaining visibility and growing your following. In this chapter, we'll delve into the intricacies of TikTok's algorithm, exploring how it works and how you can leverage it to your advantage.

UNDERSTANDING TIKTOK'S ALGORITHM

Imagine TikTok as a giant, bustling marketplace. Each user has a unique stall, filled with their creations, and the algorithm is the marketplace manager, deciding which stalls get the most foot traffic. Understanding how this manager thinks and operates is essential for ensuring your stall gets noticed. The algorithm's primary goal is to keep users engaged and entertained, showing them content they are likely to enjoy based on their behavior on the app.

TikTok's algorithm is highly sophisticated, using machine learning to analyze user interactions and preferences. Here's a deeper look at the main factors that influence the algorithm:

User Interactions

One of the most significant factors the algorithm considers is user interactions. This includes likes, comments, shares, and the time spent watching a video. The more engagement a video receives, the more likely it is to be shown to a broader audience. For instance, if users frequently like, comment on, or share your videos, the algorithm takes this as a signal that your content is engaging and worth promoting.

To leverage this, focus on creating content that encourages interaction. Ask questions in your videos, invite viewers to share their thoughts in the comments, and create content that people will want to share with their friends. The more engagement your videos generate, the more favorably the algorithm will view them.

Watch Time And Completion Rate

The amount of time users spend watching your videos and whether they watch them to the end are critical metrics for the algorithm. A high completion rate indicates that viewers find your content engaging enough to watch the entire video. This can significantly boost your video's chances of being shown to more users.

To improve your watch time and completion rate, aim to create content that captures attention quickly and holds it throughout. Start your videos with a strong hook that intrigues viewers and makes them want to keep watching. Keep your content concise and to the point, ensuring there's no dull moment that might cause viewers to scroll away.

Replays

Another metric that TikTok considers is the number of times a video is replayed. If users are watching your videos multiple times, it signals to the algorithm that your content is particularly engaging or informative. This can lead to your videos being promoted more widely.

Creating content that viewers want to rewatch can be challenging, but it's not impossible. Tutorials, tips, and visually appealing content often get replayed. For instance, if you're demonstrating how to create a specific craft, viewers might replay the video to follow along with each step. Similarly, visually stunning or clever videos might be replayed as viewers appreciate the details or share them with friends.

Shares

Shares are a strong indicator of engaging content. When users share your videos, they are essentially vouching for their quality, suggesting that their friends or followers will enjoy the content too. Shared videos get more visibility, both from the algorithm and from the direct audience of those who shared them.

To encourage shares, create content that resonates deeply with your audience. Emotional, funny, or highly relatable content tends to get shared more often. Think about what makes your audience tick and how you can create videos that they'll want to share with their network.

Comments

Comments are another vital interaction metric. They indicate that viewers are engaged enough with your content to take the time to write a response. The algorithm takes this as a positive signal and is more likely to promote videos that receive a lot of comments.

Encourage comments by asking questions, inviting opinions, or sparking discussions in your videos. Responding to comments can also increase engagement and show the algorithm that your content fosters active interaction.

Likes

While likes are a more passive form of engagement compared to comments or shares, they are still a significant factor in the algorithm. Videos with a high number of likes are more likely to be promoted, as likes indicate that users enjoyed the content.

Although likes are important, they are just one piece of the puzzle. Focus on creating high-quality content that not only gets likes but also encourages deeper forms of engagement like comments and shares.

Video Information

The algorithm also looks at the information associated with your video, such as captions, hashtags, and sounds. Captions and hashtags help the algorithm understand the content and context of your video, making it easier to match it with users who might be interested in it.

Using relevant and trending hashtags can significantly boost your video's visibility. However, avoid using too many hashtags or ones that aren't relevant to your content, as this can come across as spammy. Instead, focus on a few well-chosen hashtags that accurately represent your video's content and context.

Captions should be clear and engaging, providing additional context or inviting viewers to take action, such as liking, commenting, or sharing the video. Captions can also include keywords that help the algorithm understand your video's theme and subject matter.

- **Sounds:** TikTok's algorithm heavily favors videos that use popular or trending sounds. If a particular song or sound clip is trending, incorporating it into your video can increase its chances of being promoted. When users interact with a specific sound, the algorithm is more likely to show them other videos that use the same sound.

Stay updated on the latest trends in music and sounds on TikTok. You can find trending sounds by browsing the Discover page or keeping an eye on popular videos in your feed. Incorporating these sounds creatively into your content can help boost your video's visibility.

- **Account Information:** The algorithm also considers the account information of the user posting the video. This includes the user's location, language preference, and the type of content they typically post. This helps TikTok tailor content to users who are more likely to be interested in it.

  For example, if your Etsy shop specializes in handmade jewelry and your account regularly posts about jewelry, the algorithm will recognize this niche and is more likely to show your content to users interested in jewelry. Consistency in the type of content you post can help the algorithm better understand your niche and audience.

- **User Device and Account Settings:** TikTok's algorithm also takes into account the device and account settings of users. This includes details like the user's device type, location, and language settings. While these factors aren't something you can control, understanding that they play a role can help you tailor your content.

For instance, if your primary audience is based in a specific region, consider using trends, languages, and cultural references relevant to that area. This can make your content more relatable and engaging for your target audience.

- **Fostering Engagement:** The TikTok algorithm rewards content that fosters engagement. To leverage this, focus on creating content that encourages viewers to interact. This could be through asking questions, using call-to-action phrases, or creating challenges that invite viewers to participate. For example, you might create a crafting challenge related to your products and invite viewers to share their own creations using a specific hashtag. This not only encourages interaction but also helps build a community around your brand.

- **Regular Posting:** Consistency is key on TikTok. Regular posting helps keep your content fresh and increases your chances of being noticed by the algorithm. Develop a content calendar to plan your videos in advance and ensure you're posting regularly. This doesn't mean you need to post multiple times a day, but maintaining a steady posting schedule can help keep your audience engaged and attract new followers.

- **Monitoring Analytics:** TikTok provides analytics tools that offer valuable insights into how your videos are performing. Use these tools to track metrics like views, likes, comments, shares, and follower growth. Analyzing this data can help you understand what types of content resonate most with your audience and adjust your strategy accordingly.

For example, if you notice that videos using a specific hashtag or sound are performing better, consider incorporating those elements into future content. Likewise, if certain types of videos consistently get higher engagement, focus on creating more of that content.

- **Adapting to Trend:** TikTok is a platform driven by trends. Keeping an eye on the latest trends and adapting them to fit your brand can significantly boost your visibility. Participate in trending challenges, use popular sounds, and incorporate trending hashtags to increase your chances of being featured on the For You page.

However, it's important to stay authentic to your brand. Choose trends that align with your brand's image and values, and adapt them in a way that feels natural and genuine. Forced or inauthentic content can turn off viewers and harm your credibility.

- **Experimenting with Content:** The TikTok algorithm is constantly evolving, and what works today might not work tomorrow. Be open to experimenting with different types of content to see what resonates with your audience. Try various formats, themes, and styles to keep your content fresh and engaging.

For example, you might experiment with tutorials, behind-the-scenes looks, customer testimonials, or humorous skits. Pay attention to how your audience responds to different types of content and use this feedback to refine your strategy.

- **Building Community:** Building a community around your brand can help foster engagement and loyalty. Interact with your followers by responding to comments, participating in discussions, and showing appreciation for their support. Creating a sense of community can encourage repeat engagement and word-of-mouth promotion.
- Consider creating content that involves your followers, such as Q&A sessions, shoutouts, or featuring user-generated content. This not only makes your followers feel valued but also provides fresh and engaging content for your profile.

CHAPTER 8: CREATING ENGAGING TIKTOK CONTENT

Welcome to another exciting chapter in mastering your Etsy business through social media. This chapter focuses on creating engaging TikTok content that drives sales. We'll explore the types of videos that resonate with audiences and the power of TikTok trends and challenges. Understanding these elements can transform your TikTok presence, turning casual viewers into enthusiastic customers.

TYPES OF VIDEOS THAT DRIVE SALES

Imagine TikTok as a dynamic, ever-changing stage where your products are the stars. Each type of video you create is a performance designed to captivate your audience and inspire them to take action—whether that's visiting your Etsy shop, making a purchase, or sharing your content with their friends. Let's dive into the various types of videos that can effectively drive sales and help your business grow.

Product Showcases

One of the most straightforward and effective types of videos for driving sales is the product showcase. These videos highlight your products, showing them in detail and explaining their features and benefits. Think of them as mini-commercials for your Etsy shop.

Start by clearly presenting your product. Use good lighting and a clean background to make sure your product is the focal point. Demonstrate how the product works, its unique features, and any details that make it special. For example, if you sell handmade candles, show the process of lighting the candle, the ambiance it creates, and the beautiful design of the container.

Engage your audience by narrating the video or adding text overlays that describe what makes your product unique. Highlight the materials used, the craftsmanship involved, and any special features that set it apart from similar products. Close the video with a call to action, such as "Visit our Etsy shop to get yours today!" or "Link in bio to shop now."

Behind-the-scenes Videos

People love seeing the magic behind the curtain. Behind-the-scenes videos give your audience a glimpse into your creative process, making them feel more connected to your brand. These videos can be incredibly engaging and build a sense of authenticity and trust with your viewers.

Show how your products are made, from start to finish. For instance, if you create handmade jewelry, film the process of selecting materials, crafting the pieces, and adding the final touches. Explain the techniques you use and the care that goes into each item. This not only educates your audience but also showcases the quality and effort behind your products.

Behind-the-scenes videos can also include your workspace, tools, and even team members if you have any. Introduce your audience to the people behind the products. Share stories, challenges, and triumphs from your creative journey. These personal touches make your brand more relatable and memorable.

Customer Testimonials And Reviews

There's nothing quite as powerful as word-of-mouth marketing. Customer testimonials and reviews provide social proof that can significantly influence potential buyers. When people see others enjoying your products, they're more likely to trust your brand and make a purchase.

Ask satisfied customers to share their experiences in short videos. They can talk about why they love your products, how they use them, and the positive impact they've had. Compile these testimonials into a single video or feature them individually.

If you have permission, share user-generated content. This could be photos or videos that customers have posted on social media featuring your products. Reposting this content with proper credit not only builds community but also showcases real-life uses of your products.

Tutorials And How-to Videos

Tutorials and how-to videos are educational and engaging, making them a great way to drive sales. These videos provide value to your audience by teaching them something new while subtly promoting your products.

Create tutorials that show how to use your products or incorporate them into everyday life. For example, if you sell artisanal soaps, create a video demonstrating how to make a luxurious at-home spa experience using your products. Explain the benefits of the ingredients and why they're good for the skin.

How-to videos can also focus on broader topics related to your niche. If you sell knitting supplies, create tutorials on different knitting techniques or simple patterns. This positions you as an expert in your field and encourages viewers to purchase your products to follow along.

Unboxing And Haul Videos

Unboxing and haul videos tap into the excitement of discovering new products. These videos are popular on TikTok and can create a buzz around your brand.

Film yourself or ask influencers to unbox your products on camera. Show the packaging, the unwrapping process, and the initial reactions to the items. Highlight the care and thoughtfulness that goes into your packaging, as well as the quality of the products themselves.

Haul videos can feature a collection of products, either from your shop or a themed selection. For example, you could create a "Self-Care Haul" featuring your bath bombs, candles, and face masks. These videos can inspire viewers to purchase multiple items and increase your average order value.

Trend-Based Content

TikTok thrives on trends. Participating in trending challenges, sounds, and hashtags can significantly boost your visibility. Trends change rapidly, so staying up-to-date and adapting them to fit your brand is key.

Keep an eye on the Discover page and your For You feed to spot emerging trends. Think creatively about how you can incorporate these trends into your content while staying true to your brand. For example, if a dance challenge is trending, create a fun video of you or your team dancing while showcasing your products.

Trend-based content shows that your brand is current and relevant. It can attract a wider audience, including users who might not have discovered your shop otherwise.

THE POWER OF TIKTOK TRENDS AND CHALLENGES

TikTok trends and challenges are the heartbeat of the platform, driving engagement and viral content. They offer a powerful way to reach new audiences, increase your visibility, and ultimately drive sales. Let's explore how you can leverage these trends and challenges to benefit your Etsy shop.

Trends on TikTok can take many forms, including specific sounds, songs, dance routines, filters, or themes. Challenges are often user-created, inviting others to participate by creating their own versions of a particular video format. Both trends and challenges spread quickly, with users eager to join in and put their own spin on the concept.

The algorithm favors content that aligns with these trends, meaning videos that participate in popular challenges are more likely to be promoted on the For You page. This can lead to increased views, followers, and engagement.

To effectively use trends and challenges, you first need to identify them. Spend time exploring TikTok, paying attention to the content that repeatedly appears on your For You page. Look for common themes, sounds, or formats that are gaining traction.

The Discover page is another valuable resource for spotting trends. It highlights trending hashtags, sounds, and challenges, providing a snapshot of what's currently popular. Follow popular creators in your niche and observe the trends they're participating in. This can give you insights into what might resonate with your target audience.

101

Once you've identified a trend, think about how you can adapt it to fit your brand and products. The key is to be creative and authentic while participating in the trend. For example, if there's a trending dance challenge, you could film yourself or your team doing the dance while holding your products or in your workspace.

If a particular sound is trending, consider how you can use it to showcase your products. For instance, a popular sound might be paired with a specific type of transition or reveal. Use this to create a dramatic or humorous reveal of your latest product.

Themed challenges can also be tailored to your brand. If there's a challenge based on a specific theme, such as self-care or sustainability, create content that highlights how your products fit into that theme. Show viewers how your products can enhance their lives in the context of the challenge.

In addition to participating in existing trends, consider creating your own challenges. This can set your brand apart and create a unique engagement opportunity for your audience. A well-crafted challenge can go viral, attracting participants and increasing your brand's visibility.

Create a challenge that's simple, fun, and easy to replicate. It should be related to your products or niche to ensure it aligns with your brand. For example, if you sell crafting supplies, you might create a "DIY Challenge" where participants show off their best DIY projects using your materials.

Promote your challenge by creating an engaging and explanatory video. Use a catchy hashtag and encourage your followers to participate and share their creations. Engage with participants by liking, commenting on, and sharing their videos. This not only boosts the challenge's visibility but also builds a sense of community around your brand.

Hashtags are a powerful tool for increasing the visibility of your TikTok content. Using trending and relevant hashtags can help your videos reach a broader audience and participate in ongoing conversations.

When creating content, include a mix of popular and niche-specific hashtags. Popular hashtags can attract a wide audience, while niche hashtags help you reach users specifically interested in your products. For example, if you're showcasing a new jewelry design, you might use hashtags like #HandmadeJewelry, #EtsySeller, and #JewelryLovers, along with any trending hashtags that fit the content.

Keep an eye on hashtag trends and adapt your content to include them. This not only boosts your video's visibility but also shows that your brand is current and engaged with the TikTok community.

Engagement is key to succeeding on TikTok. Actively interacting with your audience and other creators helps build relationships and increase your visibility. Respond to comments on your videos, engage with content from other users, and participate in discussions.

Collaborating with other creators can also enhance your reach. Find influencers or creators who share a similar audience and propose a collaboration. This could be a joint challenge, a duet, or simply a shoutout. Collaborations introduce your brand to new followers and provide fresh, engaging content for both your profiles.

Consistency is crucial when building a presence on TikTok. Regularly posting content keeps your audience engaged and helps the algorithm recognize your activity, potentially boosting your videos to more viewers. However, consistency isn't just about frequency; it's also about maintaining a consistent voice and style that aligns with your brand.

Authenticity resonates deeply with TikTok users. Unlike some other platforms, TikTok thrives on genuine, relatable content. Don't be afraid to show the human side of your business. Share your successes and your struggles, celebrate milestones, and engage with your community in a real and personable way. Authenticity builds trust and connection, which are essential for converting viewers into loyal customers.

Understanding how your content performs on TikTok is crucial for continuous improvement. TikTok provides analytics tools that offer insights into your video performance, audience demographics, and engagement metrics. Use these tools to identify what types of content resonate most with your audience and which trends drive the most engagement.

Pay attention to metrics such as views, likes, comments, shares, and follower growth. Analyzing these metrics helps you understand which videos are most effective at driving engagement and sales. For instance, if you notice that tutorials and behind-the-scenes videos consistently perform well, consider creating more of this content.

Adapting your strategy based on these insights is key. If certain types of videos aren't performing as expected, experiment with different formats, styles, or topics. The TikTok landscape is constantly evolving, so staying flexible and open to new ideas will help you stay relevant and engaging.

While organic reach is a powerful tool on TikTok, incorporating paid advertising can further amplify your reach and drive sales. TikTok offers various ad formats, including in-feed ads, branded hashtags, and sponsored effects, each with unique advantages.

In-feed ads appear seamlessly in users' For You feed, offering a natural way to showcase your products. These ads can drive traffic to your TikTok profile, website, or specific product pages. Ensure your ads are engaging and visually appealing to capture viewers' attention quickly.

Branded hashtag challenges are another effective ad format. These challenges encourage users to create content around a specific hashtag, promoting engagement and user-generated content. A well-executed branded challenge can go viral, significantly boosting your brand's visibility.

Sponsored effects allow you to create custom filters or effects that users can apply to their videos. This not only promotes your brand but also encourages creative interaction from users. Sponsored effects can be particularly effective for increasing brand awareness and driving engagement.

Building a community around your brand on TikTok is more than just gaining followers; it's about fostering a sense of connection and loyalty. Engage with your audience by responding to comments, thanking followers, and showing appreciation for their support. Create content that involves your community, such as Q&A sessions, user-generated content features, or shoutouts to loyal fans.

Encourage your followers to share their experiences with your products. Create hashtags for specific campaigns or challenges and invite your audience to participate. Highlighting user-generated content not only boosts engagement but also shows that you value your customers and their creativity.

Collaborating with other TikTok creators can also help build your community. Joint challenges, duets, and shoutouts introduce your brand to new audiences and foster a sense of collaboration and community.

CRAFTING A CONTENT CALENDAR

Imagine your content calendar as a roadmap guiding your journey through the dynamic landscape of TikTok. It's your blueprint for success, helping you stay organized, inspired, and on track. Crafting a content calendar involves several steps, each crucial to building a robust TikTok strategy.

Before you start planning your content, it's essential to understand who your audience is and what they want to see. Spend some time analyzing your followers' demographics, interests, and engagement patterns. What types of content resonate most with them? What are their pain points, needs, and desires? Understanding these aspects will help you tailor your content to meet their expectations and keep them engaged.

Engage with your audience by asking questions, responding to comments, and monitoring the types of content that generate the most interaction. This ongoing dialogue will provide valuable insights into what your audience enjoys and expects from your brand.

A successful content calendar starts with clear, achievable goals. What do you want to accomplish with your TikTok presence? Are you aiming to increase brand awareness, drive traffic to your Etsy shop, boost sales, or grow your follower base? Setting specific goals helps you measure your progress and adjust your strategy as needed.

For instance, if your goal is to drive traffic to your Etsy shop, you might focus on creating product showcases, tutorials, and behind-the-scenes content that highlights your products' unique features. If you're aiming to grow your follower base, participating in trending challenges and creating shareable, engaging content might be your priority.

Variety is the spice of life, and it's no different on TikTok. Planning different content themes ensures your feed remains diverse and interesting. Content themes can include product showcases, tutorials, behind-the-scenes looks, customer testimonials, trend-based videos, and more.

Consider creating a theme for each day of the week or each week of the month. For example, you might dedicate Mondays to product showcases, Tuesdays to tutorials, Wednesdays to behind-the-scenes content, and so on. This approach not only keeps your content varied but also makes planning easier and more structured.

TikTok thrives on trends and challenges. These are the lifeblood of the platform, driving engagement and visibility. As you craft your content calendar, leave room for flexibility to incorporate these trends. Regularly check the Discover page and your For You feed to stay updated on the latest trends and challenges.

Think creatively about how you can adapt these trends to fit your brand. Whether it's a dance challenge, a popular sound, or a themed hashtag, participating in trends helps you stay relevant and increases your chances of reaching a wider audience.

Once you have your content themes and goals in place, it's time to start scheduling your content. Decide how often you want to post. Consistency is key, but so is quality. It's better to post high-quality content a few times a week than to post mediocre content daily.

Use a calendar tool to map out your content. This could be a digital calendar like Google Calendar, a project management tool like Trello or Asana, or a simple paper planner. Schedule specific days and times for each post, taking into account when your audience is most active. TikTok analytics can provide insights into the best times to post based on your followers' activity patterns.

A content pipeline helps you manage the different stages of content creation, from brainstorming ideas to posting the final video. Break down your content creation process into manageable steps, such as ideation, scripting, filming, editing, and posting.

For each scheduled post, note the current status and any upcoming tasks. This ensures that you stay organized and on track, and it allows you to see at a glance what needs to be done next. Keeping your content pipeline organized can prevent last-minute scrambles and ensure that each video is polished and ready to go when it's time to post.

Set aside regular time for brainstorming and ideation. This is where you let your creativity flow and come up with fresh, engaging ideas for your TikTok content. Look for inspiration everywhere—on TikTok itself, in your daily life, from your customers' feedback, and even from competitors.

Create a list or a board where you can jot down or pin ideas as they come. Not every idea will make it to your content calendar, but having a pool of ideas to draw from ensures you're never starting from scratch. Encourage your team, if you have one, to contribute ideas as well. Collaborative brainstorming can lead to innovative content that you might not have thought of on your own.

While some TikTok videos are spontaneous, others benefit from a bit of planning. For more complex videos, consider scripting and storyboarding your content. This doesn't mean writing a full script for every video, but having a clear outline of what you want to say and do can be incredibly helpful.

Storyboarding involves sketching out each shot of your video. This visual plan can help you organize your thoughts, ensure you don't miss any key elements, and make filming smoother. Even a simple storyboard can make a big difference in the quality of your final video.

When it's time to film, make sure you have all the necessary equipment and props ready. Use good lighting, ideally natural light, or invest in some affordable lighting equipment. Ensure your camera or smartphone is set up to capture the best angles of your product.

Editing is where your video comes to life. TikTok's in-app editing tools are powerful and user-friendly, allowing you to trim clips, add transitions, and incorporate music and effects. Spend some time experimenting with these tools to see what works best for your content. Don't rush the editing process—take the time to ensure your video is engaging and polished.

With your content ready, stick to your schedule and post regularly. But posting is just the beginning. Engage with your audience by responding to comments, liking their responses, and participating in conversations. This interaction helps build a loyal community and encourages more engagement.

Monitor the performance of your posts through TikTok analytics. Pay attention to metrics like views, likes, shares, and comments. Analyzing this data helps you understand what types of content resonate most with your audience and adjust your strategy accordingly.

At the end of each month or quarter, review your content calendar and the performance of your videos. Look at what worked well and what didn't. Did certain themes or types of videos consistently perform better? Were there any trends or challenges that drove significant engagement?

Use these insights to adapt your content calendar for the coming months. Continuously refining your strategy based on performance data ensures that your content remains fresh, engaging, and effective.

Your content calendar should also reflect seasonal trends and promotional activities. Plan ahead for holidays, special events, and sales. Seasonal content can be highly engaging as it taps into the current mood and interests of your audience.

For example, during the holiday season, you might create videos showcasing your products as perfect gifts, sharing holiday-themed tutorials, or offering special discounts. Similarly, plan content around major events in your industry or community, such as craft fairs, festivals, or Etsy promotions.

Collaborations and influencer marketing can significantly boost your reach and engagement on TikTok. Identify influencers or fellow creators in your niche who share a similar audience. Reach out to them with collaboration ideas that benefit both parties.

Collaborations can take various forms, such as joint challenges, duets, or shoutouts. These partnerships not only introduce your brand to new followers but also provide fresh content for your profile. Schedule these collaborations into your content calendar and plan the details in advance to ensure a smooth execution.

Encouraging user-generated content (UGC) is another effective strategy. Create campaigns or challenges that invite your followers to create and share their own videos featuring your products. This not only boosts engagement but also provides you with authentic, relatable content to feature on your profile.

Showcase UGC by reposting it on your account, with proper credit to the creators. This not only shows appreciation for your customers but also builds a sense of community and trust around your brand.

Educational content that provides value to your audience can establish you as an authority in your niche. Create tutorials, tips, and how-to videos that teach your followers something new. This type of content is highly shareable and can drive traffic to your profile and Etsy shop.

For example, if you sell knitting supplies, create videos teaching different knitting techniques or simple patterns. If you offer skincare products, share tips on how to use them effectively. Educational content not only engages your audience but also builds trust and credibility.

While a content calendar provides structure, it's important to leave room for experimentation and creativity. TikTok is a platform that rewards innovation and authenticity. Don't be afraid to try new things, take risks, and think outside the box.

Experiment with different video formats, styles, and themes. Test out new ideas and see how your audience responds.

Creativity and spontaneity can lead to some of your most engaging and successful content.

Maintaining a content calendar and consistently creating engaging content can be challenging. It's important to stay motivated and inspired. Surround yourself with inspiration, whether it's other TikTok creators, your own products, or the feedback from your audience.

Take breaks when needed to avoid burnout. Stepping back and recharging can help you come back with fresh ideas and renewed enthusiasm. Remember, the goal is to create content that you enjoy making and that your audience enjoys watching.

Use TikTok's analytics tools to continuously monitor and improve your content strategy. Track key metrics like views, likes, shares, comments, and follower growth. Identify patterns and trends in your content performance and use these insights to refine your approach.

For example, if you notice that certain types of videos consistently receive higher engagement, consider incorporating more of that content into your calendar. Conversely, if some videos underperform, analyze why and adjust your strategy accordingly.

TikTok is a dynamic platform that frequently updates its features and algorithms. Stay informed about any changes and adapt your strategy accordingly. Follow TikTok's official blog and social media channels to stay updated on the latest features, trends, and best practices.

Adapting to platform changes ensures that your content remains relevant and effective. Embrace new features and experiment with them to see how they can enhance your content and engagement.

Building a support system can make managing your TikTok content calendar more manageable and enjoyable. If you have a team, delegate tasks and responsibilities to ensure that everyone is contributing to the content creation process.

If you're a solo creator, consider networking with other TikTok creators or joining online communities where you can share ideas, seek advice, and offer support. Building a network of fellow creators can provide motivation, inspiration, and valuable insights.

Creating a content calendar for TikTok is an ongoing process that requires planning, creativity, and adaptability. By understanding your audience, setting clear goals, incorporating trends, and regularly reviewing your performance, you can develop a robust and effective content strategy that drives engagement and sales. With a well-crafted content calendar, you'll be well-equipped to navigate the dynamic landscape of TikTok and build a thriving presence for your Etsy business.

CHAPTER 9: TIKTOK MARKETING STRATEGIES

Welcome to the world of TikTok marketing strategies, where creativity meets data-driven decisions to maximize your reach and engagement. In this chapter, we will explore two powerful tools that can help you stand out on TikTok: leveraging hashtags and music, and using TikTok ads. These strategies will enable you to connect with a broader audience, boost your brand visibility, and ultimately drive more sales to your Etsy shop.

LEVERAGING HASHTAGS AND MUSIC

Think of hashtags and music as the lifeblood of TikTok. They are essential elements that help categorize your content, make it discoverable, and create an emotional connection with your audience. By understanding how to use these tools effectively, you can enhance your content's reach and resonance.

The Power of Hashtags

Hashtags are more than just a trend; they are a way to organize content and connect with communities on TikTok.

When you use hashtags effectively, your videos can reach users who are searching for or following those specific tags, thereby increasing your visibility.

Start by researching popular and relevant hashtags in your niche. For example, if you sell handmade jewelry, hashtags like #HandmadeJewelry, #EtsySeller, #JewelryLovers, and #Handcrafted could be relevant. Look at what other successful creators in your field are using and take note of trending hashtags. TikTok's Discover page is a great resource for identifying what's currently popular.

However, don't just use popular hashtags; balance them with niche-specific ones. This helps target a more specific audience that is genuinely interested in your products. Using too many generic hashtags can make your content get lost in the noise, while highly specific hashtags can connect you with a more engaged and relevant audience.

Craft your hashtags strategically. Include a mix of broad and specific tags, and always ensure they are relevant to your content. For instance, if you're posting a tutorial on making a beaded bracelet, you might use hashtags like #JewelryMaking, #DIYBracelet, #BeadedJewelry, and #HandmadeGift. This not only categorizes your video but also taps into multiple audiences interested in different aspects of your content.

Encourage your followers to use a branded hashtag. This creates a sense of community and makes it easier to track user-generated content. For example, you could start a hashtag like #MyHandmadeJewelry and invite customers to share their purchases or creations using your materials. Feature the best posts on your profile, giving your followers a chance to shine and feel valued.

Harnessing the Emotional Power of Music

Music is an integral part of TikTok, and choosing the right track can significantly enhance your video's appeal. The platform offers an extensive library of songs and sound effects, ranging from trending hits to niche genres. The right music can set the tone, evoke emotions, and make your content more memorable.

When selecting music, consider the mood and message of your video. Upbeat, energetic tracks can make your content feel lively and fun, while softer, more melodic tunes can create a calm, intimate atmosphere. For example, if you're showcasing a delicate piece of jewelry, a gentle, elegant background track might enhance the visual appeal and create a more immersive experience.

Trending sounds and songs are particularly powerful because they have a built-in audience. When users interact with a specific sound, they often explore other videos that use the same track. Incorporating trending music can increase your chances of appearing on the For You page and reaching a wider audience.

To find trending music, keep an eye on the Discover page and observe the sounds used in popular videos on your For You feed. TikTok also provides a list of trending sounds within the app, making it easy to see what's currently popular. Don't be afraid to experiment with different genres and styles to see what resonates best with your audience.

In addition to trending sounds, consider creating original audio content. This can be particularly effective for brand recognition. A catchy jingle, unique sound effect, or even your voice narrating a tutorial can become a signature element of your brand. Original sounds can also be used by other creators, further spreading your brand's reach.

Combining Hashtags and Music for Maximum Impact

The magic really happens when you combine the strategic use of hashtags with the emotional pull of music. Think of your video as a story, with hashtags guiding viewers to your content and music enhancing their experience. Together, they create a compelling narrative that draws people in and encourages them to engage.

For instance, if you're participating in a TikTok challenge that involves a specific dance to a trending song, use the challenge hashtag along with other relevant tags. The trending music will attract viewers participating in or following the challenge, while the hashtags will categorize your content and help it reach a broader audience.

Keep an eye on how your videos perform with different combinations of hashtags and music. TikTok's analytics can provide insights into which tags and tracks drive the most engagement. Use this data to refine your strategy, focusing on what works best for your audience.

USING TIKTOK ADS

While organic reach is a powerful tool on TikTok, using ads can significantly boost your visibility and help you achieve specific business goals, such as driving traffic to your Etsy shop or promoting a new product launch. TikTok offers several ad formats, each with unique advantages.

In-feed ads are native ads that appear in users' For You feeds, blending seamlessly with organic content. These ads can be up to 60 seconds long, though shorter ads (15 seconds or less) tend to perform better. In-feed ads support various call-to-action buttons, such as "Shop Now," "Learn More," or "Visit Website," making them ideal for driving traffic to your Etsy shop.

To create an effective in-feed ad, focus on capturing attention within the first few seconds. Use engaging visuals, compelling music, and a clear message. Highlight the unique features of your product and include a strong call to action. For example, showcase a best-selling item with close-up shots, demonstrate its use, and end with a prompt to visit your shop for more details.

TikTok's self-serve ad platform allows you to target your ads based on demographics, interests, and behaviors. Use these targeting options to reach users who are most likely to be interested in your products. Regularly monitor your ad performance and make adjustments as needed to optimize your results.

Branded hashtag challenges are a powerful way to engage users and encourage user-generated content. These challenges invite users to create their own videos around a specific theme or activity using a branded hashtag that you create. Branded hashtag challenges can generate a lot of buzz and drive significant engagement, as users get involved and share their own content, often leading to a viral effect.

To launch a branded hashtag challenge, start by crafting a clear, fun, and easy-to-follow concept. Your challenge should be related to your brand or products in a way that encourages creativity and participation. For example, if you sell handmade jewelry, you could create a challenge asking users to show off their favorite jewelry styling tips or their own handmade creations using your materials.

Once you've developed your challenge concept, create a promotional video explaining the challenge and demonstrating how to participate. Use engaging visuals, popular music, and a clear call to action to encourage viewers to join in. Make sure to showcase your products prominently in the video to highlight their connection to the challenge.

Promote your challenge by collaborating with popular TikTok creators or influencers who can help spread the word to a larger audience. These influencers can create their own videos participating in the challenge, further encouraging their followers to join in.

Monitor the progress of your hashtag challenge through TikTok's analytics. Track the number of videos created, views, likes, shares, and overall engagement. Engage with participants by liking, commenting on, and sharing their videos to keep the momentum going. This interaction helps build a community around your brand and encourages even more participation.

Branded effects allow you to create custom filters, stickers, and augmented reality (AR) effects that users can apply to their own videos. These effects can be a fun and interactive way to engage users and promote your brand.

Design branded effects that are visually appealing and relevant to your products. For example, if you sell skincare products, you could create a filter that adds a glowing skin effect, or if you offer home decor items, an AR effect that allows users to visualize your products in their space.

Promote your branded effects by creating demonstration videos showing how to use them. Encourage users to try out the effects and share their videos with your branded hashtag. This not only increases engagement but also spreads your brand's visual identity across the platform.

TopView ads are full-screen ads that appear when users first open the TikTok app. These ads can be up to 60 seconds long and are highly effective at capturing attention due to their prominent placement.

Use TopView ads to make a bold statement and showcase your most compelling content. Highlight new product launches, special promotions, or key brand messages. The full-screen format allows you to create immersive, visually striking videos that leave a lasting impression.

Due to their premium placement, TopView ads tend to be more expensive than other ad formats. However, they can deliver high visibility and engagement, making them a valuable investment for major campaigns or important announcements.

Spark Ads are a unique ad format that allows you to boost organic content, including your own posts and posts from other users that mention your brand. This format enables you to amplify content that is already performing well, increasing its reach and impact.

Identify organic posts that have high engagement and align with your marketing goals. This could be a popular video from your profile, a user-generated post featuring your products, or a collaboration with an influencer. By boosting these posts with Spark Ads, you can reach a wider audience and drive more traffic to your profile or website.

Spark Ads blend seamlessly with organic content, making them less intrusive and more engaging for viewers. They are an excellent way to leverage the authentic appeal of user-generated content while maximizing your ad spend.

Measuring and Optimizing Ad Performance

Effective ad campaigns require continuous monitoring and optimization. Use TikTok's add analytics to track key performance metrics, such as impressions, clicks, engagement rates, and conversion rates. These insights help you understand what's working and what needs improvement.

Experiment with different ad formats, targeting options, and creative elements to see what drives the best results. A/B testing can be particularly useful for comparing different versions of your ads and identifying the most effective strategies.

Regularly review your ad performance and make data-driven adjustments to optimize your campaigns. This might involve refining your targeting criteria, tweaking your creative content, or reallocating your budget to the best-performing ads.

While TikTok ads can significantly boost your visibility, it's important to integrate them seamlessly with your organic content. A well-rounded strategy combines paid advertising with organic engagement to create a cohesive brand presence.

Ensure that your ads reflect the same tone, style, and values as your organic content. This consistency helps build a strong, recognizable brand identity and makes your ads feel more authentic and relatable to viewers.

Engage with your audience through both organic posts and ads. Respond to comments, participate in conversations, and show appreciation for user-generated content. Building a genuine connection with your audience fosters loyalty and encourages long-term engagement.

TikTok is constantly evolving, with new trends, features, and updates emerging regularly. Staying informed about these changes is crucial for maintaining a competitive edge and maximizing your marketing efforts.

Follow TikTok's official blog, social media channels, and industry news sources to stay updated on the latest developments. Experiment with new features and adapt your strategy to incorporate trending content and innovative formats.

By staying agile and open to experimentation, you can keep your content fresh, relevant, and engaging, ensuring that your brand remains at the forefront of TikTok's vibrant community.

TikTok offers a dynamic and powerful platform for marketing your Etsy business. By leveraging hashtags and music effectively and using TikTok ads strategically, you can reach a broader audience, boost engagement, and drive sales. Crafting a thoughtful and data-driven approach to your TikTok marketing ensures that you stay connected with your audience and continuously grow your brand's presence in this exciting digital landscape.

COLLABORATIONS AND INFLUENCER MARKETING

Imagine TikTok as a grand stage where influencers are the stars drawing in crowds. These influencers have built trust and a loyal following through their authentic and engaging content. By collaborating with them, your brand can gain credibility and tap into their established audiences. Let's explore how to effectively engage in collaborations and influencer marketing on TikTok.

The first step in influencer marketing is identifying the right influencers for your brand. It's not just about the number of followers they have, but about finding influencers whose values align with your brand and whose audience matches your target market. Look for influencers who are passionate about topics related to your products. For example, if you sell handmade crafts, an influencer known for DIY projects or home decor would be a great fit.

Spend time on TikTok exploring different creators. Pay attention to the engagement on their posts—how many likes, comments, and shares they receive can be a good indicator of their influence. Look at the type of content they produce and how well it resonates with their audience. Authenticity and engagement often outweigh sheer follower numbers.

Once you've identified potential influencers, start building relationships with them. Follow their accounts, engage with their content by liking, commenting, and sharing. This not only puts you on their radar but also helps you understand their style and audience better.

When you're ready to reach out, craft a personalized message. Influencers receive numerous collaboration requests, so making your message stand out is crucial. Highlight why you admire their work and how your products align with their content. Be clear about what you're offering and what you hope to achieve from the collaboration. For instance, you could say, "I've been following your DIY tutorials and love your creative approach. I believe our handmade jewelry would resonate with your audience. We'd love to collaborate and provide you with some pieces for your upcoming projects. Let's discuss how we can work together to create engaging content for your followers."

Being transparent about your expectations and open to the influencer's ideas fosters a collaborative spirit. Influencers know their audience best and can offer valuable insights into what type of content will perform well.

There are various ways to collaborate with influencers on TikTok. One popular type is product reviews and unboxings. Send your products to influencers for them to review or unbox on camera. This gives their audience an authentic look at your products and builds trust. Unboxing videos are particularly engaging as they capture the influencer's genuine reactions and highlight the product's packaging and presentation.

Sponsored content is another effective collaboration method. Work with influencers to create sponsored posts that showcase your products in use. This could be a tutorial, a styling tip, or a creative project featuring your products. Ensure the content feels natural and fits seamlessly with the influencer's usual style.

Giveaways and contests are great for driving engagement and attracting new followers to your brand. Partner with influencers to host giveaways or contests. For example, you could provide products as prizes and ask followers to enter by following your account, liking the post, and tagging friends.

Collaborative challenges can significantly boost the reach of your brand. Create a branded challenge and invite influencers to participate. This can encourage user-generated content. Influencers can kick off the challenge, demonstrating how to participate and inviting their followers to join.

Live streams and Q&A sessions offer real-time engagement and can be incredibly effective. Partner with influencers for live streams where they use your products, answer questions, or discuss topics related to your brand. This real-time engagement can build a stronger connection with the audience.

To ensure your collaborations are effective, it's important to track and measure their success. Define clear goals before the collaboration—whether it's increasing brand awareness, driving traffic to your Etsy shop, or boosting sales. Use

TikTok's analytics tools to monitor key metrics such as views, likes, shares,comments, and follower growth. These metrics will give you a clear picture of how well the collaboration is performing and whether it is meeting your goals.

Engage with the content during and after the collaboration. Respond to comments, share the content on your own profile, and continue the conversation with the influencer and their audience. This ongoing engagement can extend the reach and impact of the collaboration. Reviewing the results and gathering feedback from the influencer is essential. Discuss what worked well and what could be improved. Use these insights to refine your future collaborations and build long-term relationships with influencers.

While one-off collaborations can be effective, building long-term relationships with influencers can have a more sustained impact. Long-term partnerships allow influencers to become genuine advocates for your brand, creating consistent and authentic content that resonates with their audience. Maintain open communication with influencers, show appreciation for their work, provide them with early access to new products, and involve them in your brand's journey. This fosters loyalty and encourages influencers to invest in the success of your brand.

While influencer marketing can be highly effective, it also comes with challenges. Finding the right influencers, managing collaborations, and measuring success can be complex. It's important to approach these challenges with flexibility and a willingness to learn. Be prepared for the possibility that not every collaboration will deliver the expected results. Influencer marketing involves a degree of unpredictability, and it may take time to find the perfect fit for your brand. Keep experimenting, analyzing, and refining your approach.

Transparency and authenticity are crucial in influencer marketing. Ensure that all collaborations comply with TikTok's guidelines and local regulations. Influencers should disclose sponsored content clearly to maintain trust with their audience. Discuss and agree on the terms of the collaboration upfront. This includes compensation, content ownership, and usage rights. Having a clear agreement helps prevent misunderstandings and ensures a smooth partnership.

Effective influencer marketing can have a profound impact on your brand. By leveraging the reach and credibility of influencers, you can connect with a larger audience, build trust, and drive sales. Influencers can bring a fresh perspective and creative approach to your content, making your brand more relatable and engaging. As you build and execute your influencer marketing strategy, stay true to your brand values and focus on creating meaningful, authentic connections. Collaborations should enhance your brand's story and resonate with your audience, contributing to a positive and memorable experience.

Influencer marketing should be a part of your broader marketing strategy. Integrate it with other efforts such as social media campaigns, email marketing, and content creation to create a cohesive and comprehensive approach.

Use the insights gained from influencer collaborations to inform other areas of your marketing. For example, if a particular type of content performs well in an influencer partnership, consider incorporating similar themes into your own posts.

By seamlessly integrating influencer marketing with your overall strategy, you create a unified brand presence that maximizes your reach and impact across different channels. In the dynamic and fast-paced world of TikTok, collaborations and influencer marketing offer powerful tools to elevate your brand and connect with your target audience. By finding the right influencers, crafting meaningful collaborations, and continuously refining your approach, you can harness the full potential of TikTok's vibrant community to grow your Etsy business and achieve your marketing goals.

Building a strong, collaborative network on TikTok requires patience, effort, and a willingness to adapt. By being proactive, maintaining open lines of communication, and focusing on creating genuine value for both your brand and your collaborators, you set the stage for successful partnerships. This collaborative approach not only enhances your marketing efforts but also contributes to the overall growth and sustainability of your business.

CHAPTER 10: BUILDING YOUR BRAND ON TIKTOK

TikTok is more than just a platform for sharing fun videos; it's a powerful tool for building a strong, recognizable brand. Establishing your brand voice and engaging with your audience are crucial steps in creating a loyal following and driving sales on TikTok. Let's explore how to create a compelling brand presence that resonates with your audience and keeps them coming back for more.

ESTABLISHING YOUR BRAND VOICE

Imagine your brand voice as the personality of your business. It's how you communicate with your audience, the tone you use, and the values you express. Establishing a clear and consistent brand voice is essential for building trust and recognition on TikTok. Your brand voice should reflect who you are as a business and what you stand for.

Start by defining your brand's core values and mission. What makes your business unique? What do you want your audience to feel when they interact with your content? Whether your brand is fun and playful, sophisticated and elegant, or eco-conscious and ethical, your voice should align with these qualities.

Think about the language and tone that best represents your brand. If your business focuses on handmade crafts, a warm, friendly, and approachable tone might be appropriate. On the other hand, if you sell high-end jewelry, a more refined and polished tone could be better suited. The key is to be authentic and true to your brand's identity.

Once you've defined your brand voice, maintain consistency across all your content. Every caption, comment, and video should reflect this voice. Consistency helps build a cohesive brand image and makes your content instantly recognizable. When your audience knows what to expect from you, they're more likely to engage and stay loyal to your brand.

Creating a content style guide can be helpful in maintaining this consistency. This guide should outline your brand's tone, language, and visual style. It can include specific phrases or hashtags you frequently use, guidelines for video production, and instructions for responding to comments. Having a clear reference can ensure that everyone involved in creating your content stays aligned with your brand voice.

Your brand voice should also be adaptable to different contexts and trends on TikTok. While consistency is important, being too rigid can make your content feel out of touch. Stay current with TikTok trends and find ways to incorporate them into your content while staying true to your brand. For example, participating in a trending challenge or using a popular sound can show that your brand is relevant and engaged with the platform's culture.

Visual elements are another key aspect of your brand voice. Consistent use of colors, fonts, and graphics can reinforce your brand's identity. Create a visual style that complements your tone and values. For instance, if your brand is eco-friendly, you might use natural, earthy colors and simple, clean designs. If your brand is vibrant and fun, bold colors and playful graphics could be more appropriate.

Storytelling is a powerful tool for expressing your brand voice. Share the story behind your business, the inspiration for your products, and the values that drive you. Authentic stories resonate with audiences and create a deeper connection with your brand. Use your videos to tell these stories, whether it's through behind-the-scenes content, customer testimonials, or personal anecdotes.

Building a recognizable brand voice on TikTok also involves being responsive and engaging with your audience. This brings us to the next crucial aspect of building your brand on TikTok: engaging with your audience.

ENGAGING WITH YOUR AUDIENCE

Engagement is the lifeblood of TikTok. It's what turns viewers into followers and followers into loyal customers. Engaging with your audience means actively participating in conversations, responding to comments, and creating content that invites interaction.

Start by making your content interactive. Ask questions, create polls, and encourage viewers to share their opinions. This not only boosts engagement but also provides valuable insights into your audience's preferences and interests. For example, you could ask your followers what new product they'd like to see next or how they use your existing products in their daily lives.

Responding to comments is a simple yet powerful way to engage with your audience. Acknowledge their input, answer their questions, and show appreciation for their support. This two-way interaction builds a sense of community and makes your followers feel valued. When they see that you're attentive and responsive, they're more likely to engage with your future content.

Creating content that showcases your followers can also boost engagement. Feature user-generated content, highlight customer testimonials, and give shoutouts to loyal followers. This not only provides social proof but also makes your audience feel involved and appreciated. For instance, if a customer shares a video of them using your product, repost it on your profile with a thank-you message.

Live streaming is another effective way to engage with your audience in real-time. Use live sessions to host Q&A segments, product demonstrations, or behind-the-scenes tours. Live streams create a sense of immediacy and intimacy, allowing you to interact with your audience on a personal level. Encourage viewers to ask questions and participate in the conversation during the live session.

Collaborating with other TikTok creators can also enhance your engagement. Partner with influencers or fellow creators who share your audience's interests. Collaborative content can introduce your brand to new followers and provide fresh, engaging content for your existing audience. For example, you could collaborate on a DIY project, a challenge, or a product review.

Consistency in posting is key to maintaining engagement. Develop a content calendar to ensure you're regularly posting new and varied content. This keeps your audience engaged and eager for more. However, quality should always take precedence over quantity. Focus on creating high-quality content that aligns with your brand voice and values.

Engagement isn't just about generating likes and comments; it's about building relationships. Show genuine interest in your audience and make them feel like part of your brand's journey. Share behind-the-scenes moments, celebrate milestones, and involve your followers in decision-making processes. For example, you could ask them to vote on a new product design or share ideas for upcoming content.

Tracking your engagement metrics is crucial for understanding what resonates with your audience. Use TikTok's analytics tools to monitor views, likes, shares, comments, and follower growth. Analyzing these metrics helps you identify successful content and refine your strategy. Pay attention to patterns and trends in your engagement data to continuously improve your approach.

Adapting to feedback is an important part of engaging with your audience. Listen to what your followers are saying and be willing to make changes based on their input. If they express a desire for different types of content or new product features, take their feedback seriously and show that you're responsive to their needs.

Authenticity is at the heart of effective engagement. Be genuine in your interactions and stay true to your brand's identity. Audiences can quickly sense when a brand is being inauthentic, which can erode trust and engagement. Share your passion, be transparent, and connect with your audience on a human level.

Creating engaging content that resonates with your audience requires creativity and a deep understanding of what makes them tick. Experiment with different content formats, themes, and styles to see what works best. Keep your content fresh and relevant by staying updated with TikTok trends and incorporating them into your strategy.

Engaging with your audience on TikTok is an ongoing process that requires time, effort, and dedication. The rewards, however, are well worth it. By building strong relationships, fostering a sense of community, and maintaining an authentic brand voice, you can create a loyal and engaged following that supports your business and helps it grow.

TikTok offers a unique and powerful platform for building your brand. Establishing a clear and consistent brand voice, combined with actively engaging with your audience, sets the foundation for a thriving presence on the platform. As you continue to develop your brand on TikTok, keep exploring new ways to connect with your followers, showcase your products, and tell your story.

Engagement goes beyond just responding to comments or creating interactive content. It's about fostering a sense of belonging among your followers. Create content that resonates emotionally with your audience. Share your brand's journey, the challenges you've overcome, and the milestones you've achieved. These stories create a deeper connection with your audience, making them feel like they're part of your brand's success.

Incorporating user-generated content (UGC) is a powerful way to build community and engagement. Encourage your customers to share videos of themselves using your products and tag your brand. Repost these videos on your profile, giving credit to the creators. This not only shows appreciation for your customers but also provides authentic content that can inspire others to engage with your brand.

Hosting contests and challenges is another effective strategy for boosting engagement. Create fun and creative challenges that encourage your followers to participate. For example, if you sell handmade crafts, you could host a challenge where followers create their own DIY projects using your materials.

Offer prizes or features for the best entries to incentivize participation.

Regularly feature your customers and followers in your content. Highlight their stories, share their testimonials, and show how they use your products in their daily lives. This not only builds a sense of community but also provides social proof that can influence potential customers.

Collaborations with other creators can significantly expand your reach and engagement. Partner with influencers or brands that share a similar audience. Collaborative content can introduce your brand to new followers and provide fresh perspectives. For example, you could collaborate on a joint DIY project, a product review, or a themed challenge. These partnerships can bring new energy to your content and attract a wider audience.

Engagement also involves listening to your audience and being responsive to their feedback. Pay attention to the comments, messages, and suggestions you receive. Use this feedback to improve your products, content, and overall brand experience. Show your audience that you value their input by making changes based on their suggestions and acknowledging their contributions.

Staying updated with TikTok trends is crucial for maintaining relevance and engagement. Regularly explore the Discover page and follow popular creators to see what's trending. Adapt these trends to fit your brand and incorporate them into your content strategy. Participating in trends shows that your brand is current and engaged with the TikTok community.

Creating a content calendar is essential for maintaining consistency and ensuring a steady flow of engaging content. Plan your content ahead of time, incorporating a mix of product showcases, tutorials, behind-the-scenes looks, and interactive posts. Having a content calendar helps you stay organized and ensures you're consistently providing value to your audience.

Analyze your engagement metrics to understand what types of content resonate most with your audience. Use TikTok's analytics tools to track views, likes, comments, shares, and follower growth. Identify patterns and trends in your engagement data and use these insights to refine your content strategy. Experiment with different content formats and themes to see what drives the most engagement.

Engagement isn't just about the quantity of interactions but also the quality. Focus on building meaningful connections with your followers. Show genuine interest in their stories, respond thoughtfully to their comments, and create content that adds value to their lives. Authenticity and sincerity go a long way in building trust and loyalty.

Remember that building a brand on TikTok is an ongoing process that requires dedication, creativity, and adaptability. Stay true to your brand's values and mission, and let your passion shine through in everything you do. Engage with your audience authentically, listen to their feedback, and continuously strive to improve their experience with your brand.

As you continue to grow your presence on TikTok, keep exploring new ways to connect with your audience, showcase your products, and tell your brand's story. The dynamic and interactive nature of TikTok offers endless opportunities to engage with your followers and build a thriving community around your brand. Embrace the journey, enjoy the creative process, and watch your brand flourish on TikTok.

GROWING YOUR FOLLOWER BASE

Imagine your TikTok profile as a bustling storefront on a busy street. The more inviting and engaging your display, the more passersby will be drawn in. Growing your follower base starts with making a strong first impression. When potential followers land on your profile, they should immediately understand what your brand is about and feel compelled to hit the follow button.

The first step is creating a visually appealing and cohesive profile. Use a high-quality profile picture that represents your brand, whether it's your logo, a product image, or a picture of yourself if you're the face of your brand. Your bio should be concise and informative, highlighting what makes your brand unique. Include a call-to-action that encourages viewers to follow you for more content related to your niche.

141

Your content is the heart of your TikTok presence. To grow your follower base, focus on creating high-quality, engaging videos that resonate with your target audience. Understand what types of content your audience enjoys and tailor your videos accordingly. This might include tutorials, behind-the-scenes looks, product showcases, or entertaining clips that align with your brand's voice and values.

Consistency is key when it comes to growing your followers. Develop a content schedule and stick to it. Regularly posting new videos keeps your audience engaged and encourages them to check back frequently for new content. However, balance is important to ensure that the quality of your content doesn't suffer in the quest for quantity.

Trends play a significant role on TikTok, and leveraging them can boost your visibility. Stay updated on the latest trends by exploring the Discover page and observing popular videos on your For You feed. Participate in trends that align with your brand, putting your unique spin on them. This not only increases your chances of being featured on the For You page but also shows that your brand is current and engaged with the TikTok community.

Engagement is crucial for growing your follower base. Actively interact with your audience by responding to comments, liking their responses, and participating in conversations. Show appreciation for your followers by acknowledging their support and featuring user-generated content. This two-way interaction builds a sense of community and loyalty, encouraging viewers to follow and stay engaged with your brand.

Collaborations with other TikTok creators can significantly expand your reach. Partner with influencers or brands that share a similar audience. Collaborative content can introduce your brand to new followers and provide fresh perspectives. For example, you could collaborate on a joint DIY project, a product review, or a themed challenge. These partnerships can bring new energy to your content and attract a wider audience.

Hashtags are another powerful tool for growing your follower base. Use a mix of popular and niche-specific hashtags to increase the discoverability of your videos. Popular hashtags can attract a broad audience, while niche hashtags help you reach viewers who are specifically interested in your content. Research relevant hashtags in your industry and include them in your posts to maximize visibility.

Engaging with trends and challenges can also boost your follower count. Create content that participates in popular challenges or uses trending sounds. These trends have built-in audiences that can significantly increase your reach. Be creative in how you incorporate trends into your content, ensuring that it still aligns with your brand's identity.

Cross-promotion is an effective strategy for growing your TikTok followers. Promote your TikTok account on other social media platforms, such as Instagram, Facebook, and Twitter. Encourage your followers on these platforms to follow you on TikTok for exclusive content. You can also embed TikTok videos on your website or blog to attract viewers from different channels.

Analyzing your TikTok analytics is crucial for understanding what works and what doesn't. Use TikTok's built-in analytics tools to track metrics such as views, likes, shares, comments, and follower growth. Identify patterns in your most successful videos and use these insights to refine your content strategy. Experiment with different formats, themes, and posting times to see what drives the most engagement.

Engaging in TikTok communities can also help you grow your follower base. Join TikTok groups or participate in niche-specific communities where you can connect with like-minded creators and viewers. Share your content, collaborate with other members, and engage in discussions. Building relationships within these communities can increase your visibility and attract new followers.

Running TikTok ads is another way to boost your follower count. TikTok offers various ad formats, including in-feed ads, branded hashtag challenges, and TopView ads. These ads can significantly increase your reach and visibility. Create compelling ads that showcase your brand's unique qualities and encourage viewers to follow you. Use targeting options to reach users who are likely to be interested in your content.

Live streaming is a powerful tool for engaging with your audience and growing your followers. Host live sessions where you interact with your viewers in real-time, answer their questions, and showcase your products. Live streams create a sense of immediacy and intimacy, making viewers feel more connected to your brand. Promote your live sessions in advance to attract a larger audience.

Creating shareable content is key to expanding your reach. Focus on making videos that viewers will want to share with their friends and followers. This could be content that's funny, inspirational, informative, or emotionally resonant. The more your videos are shared, the more visibility you'll gain, and the more likely you are to attract new followers.

Authenticity is crucial for building a loyal follower base. Be genuine in your interactions and stay true to your brand's values. Audiences can quickly sense when a brand is being inauthentic, which can erode trust and engagement. Share your passion, be transparent, and connect with your audience on a human level.

Growing your follower base on TikTok is an ongoing process that requires dedication, creativity, and adaptability. Stay true to your brand's values and mission, and let your passion shine through in everything you do. Engage with your audience authentically, listen to their feedback, and continuously strive to improve their experience with your brand.

Embrace the journey of growing your TikTok followers. Enjoy the creative process, experiment with new ideas, and celebrate the milestones along the way. As you build a loyal and engaged follower base, you'll create a thriving community that supports your brand and helps it grow. The dynamic and interactive nature of TikTok offers endless opportunities to connect with your audience and build a successful presence on the platform.

CHAPTER 11: LINKING TIKTOK TO YOUR ETSY SHOP

In the vibrant world of TikTok, where creativity and engagement flourish, one of your primary goals as a business owner is to convert your viewers into customers. This transformation hinges on how effectively you link your TikTok profile to your Etsy shop. By adding clickable links and creating compelling call-to-actions (CTAs), you can guide your audience seamlessly from watching your videos to purchasing your products. Let's delve into these crucial strategies to ensure your TikTok efforts translate into tangible sales for your Etsy shop.

ADDING CLICKABLE LINKS

Imagine your TikTok profile as a gateway to your Etsy shop. Adding clickable links is akin to laying down a path that leads your audience directly to your storefront. However, TikTok doesn't allow clickable links in video descriptions, making your profile and bio the primary places to include them.

Start by ensuring your TikTok profile is optimized. Your bio should clearly communicate what your brand is about and what value you offer. Within this space, include a direct, clickable link to your Etsy shop. Use a URL shortener to create a clean, concise link that's easy to read and remember. For example, a link like bit.ly/MyEtsyShop is more user-friendly than a long, complicated URL.

Consider using a link-in-bio tool like Linktree or similar services. These tools allow you to create a single link that houses multiple destinations. When a user clicks on your bio link, they're taken to a landing page with several clickable buttons, directing them to different parts of your Etsy shop, social media profiles, or other relevant pages. This approach maximizes the utility of your single bio link, offering your audience a variety of options.

When crafting your bio, make it compelling. Explain why viewers should click on your link. For example, instead of simply stating "Visit my Etsy shop," you could say, "Discover handcrafted jewelry and exclusive offers at my Etsy shop. Click the link below!" This not only informs but also entices your audience to take action.

To reinforce the presence of your link, mention it frequently in your videos. For instance, when showcasing a new product, conclude by inviting viewers to visit your Etsy shop via the link in your bio. Phrases like "Check out the link in my bio for more details" or "Tap the link in my bio to shop now" make it easy for viewers to transition from watching your video to exploring your shop.

Another effective strategy is to use TikTok's paid promotion features. With a Pro Account, you can create ads that include clickable links directly within the video. These ads can drive traffic straight to your Etsy shop without the extra step of going through your bio link. Utilize in-feed ads, branded hashtag challenges, or TopView ads to feature your products with direct links, enhancing the shopping experience for your audience.

Regularly update the link in your bio to reflect current promotions, new product launches, or special events. Keeping your link relevant encourages repeat clicks from returning visitors. Announce these updates in your videos to alert your audience to new opportunities, maintaining their interest and engagement.

CREATING EFFECTIVE CALL-TO-ACTIONS

While clickable links pave the way for traffic, effective call-to-actions (CTAs) are the signposts guiding your audience down the path. A strong CTA can significantly boost the chances of converting viewers into customers. It's about prompting your audience to take the desired action with clear, compelling, and concise messages.

Begin by understanding the psychology behind a good CTA. A successful CTA addresses a need or desire of your audience and presents your product as the solution. It's not just about telling people what to do; it's about making them want to do it.

In your TikTok videos, use CTAs to direct viewers to specific actions. This could be visiting your Etsy shop, signing up for a newsletter, or following your account. The language you use should be straightforward and action-oriented. For example, instead of saying "You might want to check out my shop," say "Visit my Etsy shop now for exclusive deals!" The latter is more direct and motivates immediate action.

Integrate your CTAs naturally into your content. Whether you're demonstrating a product, sharing a tutorial, or telling a story, find moments to seamlessly introduce your CTA. For example, if you're showing how to use a handmade soap, end with, "Want to experience this for yourself? Tap the link in my bio to get yours today!" This keeps the viewer engaged and lessens the chance of them feeling like they're being sold to.

Vary your CTAs to keep your content fresh and engaging. Sometimes invite viewers to "Swipe up to shop" if you're using TikTok's ad features, or "Comment below if you have any questions about this product." Different CTAs can help achieve various goals, whether it's driving sales, increasing engagement, or gathering feedback.

Leveraging urgency and exclusivity in your CTAs can also be highly effective. Phrases like "Limited time offer!" or "Only a few items left!" create a sense of urgency that can prompt viewers to act quickly. Similarly, "Exclusive discount for TikTok followers—link in bio!" makes your audience feel special and valued, encouraging them to take advantage of the offer.

Engaging your audience through interactive CTAs can also drive traffic and sales. Host giveaways or challenges that require viewers to visit your Etsy shop or follow your account. For instance, you could say, "Enter our giveaway by following us and visiting our Etsy shop via the link in my bio!" This not only increases traffic but also boosts your follower count and engagement.

Tracking the effectiveness of your CTAs is crucial for refining your strategy. Use TikTok's analytics to monitor the performance of your videos and see which CTAs are driving the most traffic and conversions. Pay attention to metrics like click-through rates, engagement rates, and conversion rates. This data will help you understand what resonates with your audience and adjust your approach accordingly.

Regularly test and optimize your CTAs to find what works best for your audience. Experiment with different phrases, placements, and tones. For example, try variations like "Discover more in my Etsy shop" versus "Shop now at my Etsy store." Analyze the results and use the insights to continually improve your CTAs.

Creating a strong CTA also involves visual cues. Use text overlays in your videos to highlight your CTA. For instance, while you're speaking your CTA, include a text overlay that says, "Tap the link in my bio to shop now!" This reinforces the message and makes it more likely to stick with your viewers.

Encourage your audience to share your content and spread the word. Ask them to tag friends who might be interested in your products or to share your videos with their followers. This organic reach can bring in new followers and potential customers who trust recommendations from their friends.

Building trust and rapport with your audience enhances the effectiveness of your CTAs. Be genuine and transparent in your interactions. Show behind-the-scenes footage, share your brand story, and engage authentically with your followers. When your audience feels connected to you and your brand, they're more likely to respond positively to your CTAs.

Maintaining a balance between promotional and non-promotional content is key. If every video you post includes a hard sell, your audience might feel overwhelmed and disengage. Mix in content that provides value, entertains, or educates without directly promoting your products. This approach builds goodwill and keeps your audience interested in your content.

Remember that building a successful TikTok presence and driving traffic to your Etsy shop is a marathon, not a sprint. Consistency, creativity, and genuine engagement are your allies in this journey. Keep experimenting with new ideas, stay responsive to your audience's needs, and enjoy the process of connecting with your community.

USING TIKTOK ANALYTICS TO IMPROVE PERFORMANCE

Welcome to the fascinating world of TikTok analytics, where data becomes the key to unlocking your brand's full potential on this dynamic platform. Just as an artist refines their craft through constant practice and feedback, you can fine-tune your TikTok strategy by understanding and leveraging the rich insights provided by TikTok analytics. This chapter will guide you through the process of using these tools to enhance your performance, drive more traffic to your Etsy shop, and create content that resonates deeply with your audience.

Understanding TikTok Analytics

Imagine TikTok analytics as a treasure map, revealing where your hidden opportunities lie. These insights can tell you what types of content your audience loves, when they're most active, and how they're engaging with your videos. By analyzing this data, you can make informed decisions that optimize your content strategy and boost your overall performance.

To start, ensure you have a TikTok Pro account, which gives you access to the platform's analytics tools. Once you've upgraded, you'll find a wealth of information categorized into different sections, each providing a unique perspective on your performance. Let's break down these sections and explore how to use them effectively.

Overview Section

The Overview section offers a snapshot of your overall performance over a selected period, typically the last seven or 28 days. Here, you'll find metrics such as total video views, follower growth, profile views, and engagement rates. This high-level view is crucial for tracking your progress and identifying trends over time.

Start by examining your total video views. This metric shows how many times your content has been watched. A steady increase in video views indicates growing interest in your content. If you notice a sudden spike, analyze which videos contributed to this growth and consider creating more similar content.

Next, look at your follower growth. This metric tells you how many new followers you've gained over the selected period. A consistent upward trend suggests that your content is resonating with viewers and encouraging them to follow your account. If your follower growth stalls or declines, it might be time to reassess your content strategy and experiment with new ideas.

Profile views offer insights into how many people are visiting your profile after watching your videos. High profile views indicate that viewers are interested in learning more about you and your brand. To capitalize on this interest, ensure your profile is optimized with a compelling bio and a clear link to your Etsy shop.

Engagement rates, which include likes, comments, shares, and saves, are critical for understanding how your audience interacts with your content. High engagement rates signify that your videos are sparking interest and conversation. Pay attention to which types of content generate the most engagement and aim to replicate those elements in future videos.

Content Section

The Content section dives deeper into the performance of individual videos. Here, you can see detailed metrics for each post, such as views, likes, comments, shares, average watch time, and traffic sources. Analyzing these metrics helps you understand what's working and what's not at a granular level.

Start by identifying your top-performing videos. Look for patterns in these videos—are they tutorials, product showcases, or behind-the-scenes glimpses? Do they feature a particular trend or sound? Understanding what makes these videos successful can inform your future content strategy.

Average watch time is a crucial metric that indicates how long viewers are staying engaged with your video. Higher average watch times suggest that your content is captivating and holding viewers' attention. Aim to create videos that capture interest within the first few seconds and maintain it throughout.

Traffic sources reveal how viewers are finding your videos. Are they coming from the For You page, your profile, or hashtags? This information can guide your promotion strategies. For instance, if a significant portion of your traffic comes from hashtags, continue using and experimenting with relevant hashtags to boost visibility.

Comments and shares are strong indicators of engagement and can provide qualitative insights into what resonates with your audience. Read through the comments to understand viewers' thoughts, questions, and feedback. Shares indicate that viewers find your content valuable enough to share with others, amplifying your reach.

Followers Section

The Followers section provides demographic insights about your audience, including age, gender, and geographic location. Understanding who your followers are helps tailor your content to their preferences and needs. This section also shows when your followers are most active, allowing you to post at optimal times for maximum engagement.

Examine the age and gender distribution of your followers. Are you reaching your target demographic? If not, consider adjusting your content to better appeal to the desired audience. For example, if you're targeting young adults but notice a large portion of your followers are older, you might need to tweak your content's tone, style, or topics.

Geographic insights show where your followers are located. This information is particularly useful for tailoring content to regional interests and timing. If you have a significant number of followers from a particular country, consider incorporating elements that resonate with that audience, such as cultural references or local trends.

Activity data reveals when your followers are most active on TikTok. Posting during these peak times increases the likelihood of your content being seen and engaged with. Experiment with posting at different times to find the sweet spot that maximizes your reach and interaction.

USING INSIGHTS TO IMPROVE PERFORMANCE

Armed with this wealth of data, the next step is to translate insights into action. Use your analytics to refine your content strategy, experiment with new ideas, and continuously improve your performance.

For instance, if your analytics reveal that tutorial videos perform exceptionally well, consider creating a series of tutorials that showcase different aspects of your products. Highlight unique features, demonstrate creative uses, and offer tips that add value to your audience. These videos not only engage viewers but also position your brand as an authority in your niche.

If your average watch time is lower than desired, focus on creating more engaging intros. Capture viewers' attention within the first few seconds with intriguing visuals, compelling questions, or eye-catching graphics. Maintain this

157

interest by delivering valuable content that keeps them watching until the end.

Use traffic source data to optimize your promotional strategies. If hashtags are driving significant traffic, research trending and relevant hashtags to include in your posts. Experiment with different combinations to see which ones yield the best results. Similarly, if the For You page is a major traffic source, continue creating content that aligns with TikTok trends and appeals to a broader audience.

Leverage comments and shares to understand what resonates with your audience. Engage with commenters, answer their questions, and thank them for their support. This not only builds a sense of community but also provides valuable feedback that can guide your content creation. Encourage viewers to share your videos by creating content that's entertaining, informative, and share-worthy.

Experimentation is key to optimizing your TikTok performance. Use A/B testing to compare different versions of your content and see which performs better. For example, you could create two versions of a product showcase video, each with a different intro, and analyze which one generates higher engagement. Continuously iterate based on your findings to refine your approach.

Tracking the performance of your CTAs is crucial for driving traffic to your Etsy shop. Use TikTok analytics to monitor the effectiveness of different CTAs in your videos. Analyze which phrases, placements, and formats generate the most clicks and conversions. For example, compare the performance of "Visit my Etsy shop via the link in my bio" versus "Tap the link in my bio to shop now." Use this data to optimize your CTAs and drive more traffic to your shop.

Consistency is vital for maintaining and growing your audience. Develop a content calendar based on your analytics insights, ensuring a regular posting schedule that aligns with your followers' activity patterns. Plan a mix of content types, including tutorials, behind-the-scenes looks, product showcases, and interactive posts. This variety keeps your audience engaged and excited for your next video.

Regularly review and update your content strategy based on your analytics. Set specific goals, such as increasing average watch time, boosting engagement rates, or driving more traffic to your Etsy shop. Use your analytics data to track your progress toward these goals and adjust your strategy as needed. Celebrate your successes and learn from any setbacks, continuously striving for improvement.

TikTok analytics is not just about numbers; it's about understanding your audience and creating content that resonates with them. Use these insights to tell compelling stories, showcase your products in innovative ways, and build a loyal community around your brand. As you master the art of leveraging TikTok analytics, you'll find that your efforts on the platform translate into meaningful growth for your Etsy shop.

The journey of linking TikTok to your Etsy shop is an ongoing process of learning, experimenting, and refining. By harnessing the power of TikTok analytics, you can make informed decisions that drive engagement, attract followers, and convert viewers into loyal customers. Embrace the dynamic nature of TikTok, stay responsive to your audience's needs, and enjoy the creative process as you build a thriving presence on this exciting platform.

CHAPTER 11: CONVERTING TIKTOK TRAFFIC TO ETSY SALES

INTEGRATING TIKTOK CONTENT WITH ETSY LISTINGS

In the fast-paced, visually driven world of TikTok, your content serves as a powerful magnet, drawing viewers in with creativity and authenticity. However, the ultimate goal is to guide these captivated viewers from their TikTok feeds to your Etsy shop, transforming interest into sales. One of the most effective ways to achieve this is by seamlessly integrating your TikTok content with your Etsy listings. This chapter explores how to create a harmonious connection between your TikTok videos and Etsy product pages, making the transition smooth and compelling for your audience.

Bridging the Gap Between TikTok and Etsy

Imagine TikTok as the front porch of your brand—it's where first impressions are made, and curiosity is piqued. Etsy, on the other hand, is the cozy interior where visitors can explore and purchase your products. Bridging the gap between these two spaces involves creating a consistent and engaging narrative that flows naturally from your TikTok content to your Etsy listings.

The first step in this process is to ensure that your TikTok content aligns with your Etsy offerings. Each video should serve as a teaser, a behind-the-scenes look, or a demonstration of the products available in your Etsy shop. This creates a cohesive brand experience that feels natural and inviting.

Showcasing Products on TikTok

On TikTok, your videos should highlight the unique features and benefits of your products in a way that's engaging and visually appealing. Use storytelling to weave a narrative around your products. For example, if you sell handmade jewelry, create a series of videos showing the process of crafting each piece—from selecting the materials to the final polish. Share the inspiration behind your designs and the care that goes into each item.

Engaging tutorials are another effective way to showcase your products. Demonstrate how to use your items, offer styling tips, or create DIY projects that feature your products. This not only provides value to your audience but also shows them the practical applications of your products in their everyday lives.

User-generated content can also play a significant role. Encourage your customers to share videos of themselves using your products and feature these videos on your TikTok profile. This provides social proof and builds a sense of

162

community around your brand. It also allows potential customers to see real-life applications and testimonials for your products.

Creating a Seamless Transition

To effectively drive traffic from TikTok to your Etsy shop, the transition must be seamless. Your TikTok profile should act as a gateway to your Etsy listings, guiding viewers effortlessly to your shop. Start by optimizing your TikTok bio with a clear, compelling link to your Etsy shop. Consider using a link-in-bio tool to provide multiple links, directing users to specific product categories, new arrivals, or special promotions.

In your videos, use strong call-to-actions (CTAs) that encourage viewers to visit your Etsy shop. Be direct and specific in your language. For example, if you're showcasing a new product, end the video with a phrase like, "Love this necklace? Click the link in my bio to get yours now!" This clear directive reduces friction and guides viewers to the next step.

Visual cues in your videos can also reinforce your CTAs. Use text overlays, arrows, or animations to draw attention to the action you want viewers to take. This visual reinforcement makes your CTA more noticeable and memorable, increasing the likelihood of conversion.

Enhancing Etsy Listings with TikTok Content

Integrating TikTok content directly into your Etsy listings can enhance the shopping experience and provide additional context for your products. Etsy allows you to include videos and multiple images in your product listings. Take advantage of this feature by embedding TikTok videos that showcase your products in action.

For instance, if you have a TikTok video demonstrating how to use one of your products, embed it in the corresponding Etsy listing. This provides potential customers with a richer understanding of the product and its uses. It also adds a dynamic element to your listing, making it more engaging than static images alone.

Use high-quality images and videos to create a visually appealing and informative product page. Show different angles, close-ups, and various uses of the product. The goal is to provide as much detail as possible, helping customers feel confident in their purchase decision.

In your product descriptions, reference your TikTok content to create a sense of continuity. For example, if a product was featured in a popular TikTok video, mention this in the description and encourage customers to check out your TikTok profile for more behind-the-scenes content and tutorials. This not only drives traffic back to your TikTok but also reinforces the connection between your social media presence and your Etsy shop.

Leveraging TikTok Trends and Hashtags

Staying current with TikTok trends and hashtags can significantly boost your visibility and drive traffic to your Etsy shop. Participate in trending challenges or use popular sounds to create videos that align with your brand. This not only increases the likelihood of your videos being featured on the For You page but also helps you reach a broader audience.

When creating trend-based content, always tie it back to your products. For example, if there's a trending dance challenge, incorporate your products into the dance routine. If a particular sound is popular, use it as a backdrop for a product showcase. The key is to make the trend work for your brand, rather than forcing your brand into the trend.

Utilize relevant hashtags to increase the discoverability of your videos. Research popular and niche-specific hashtags related to your products and industry. Including these hashtags in your posts helps you reach users who are interested in those topics, increasing the chances of attracting potential customers.

Engaging with Your Audience

Engagement is crucial for building a loyal customer base and driving sales. Actively interact with your audience by responding to comments, answering questions, and participating in conversations. Show appreciation for your followers by acknowledging their support and featuring user-generated content.

Host live streams on TikTok to engage with your audience in real time. Use these sessions to showcase new products, offer exclusive discounts, and answer questions from viewers. Live streams create a sense of urgency and excitement, encouraging viewers to make immediate purchases.

Encourage viewers to share their experiences with your products by hosting giveaways or challenges. For example, you could create a challenge where customers share videos of how they use your products in their daily lives. Offer a prize for the best entry to incentivize participation. This not only generates user-generated content but also increases brand visibility and engagement.

Optimizing the Customer Journey

The customer journey from TikTok to Etsy should be smooth and intuitive. Ensure that your Etsy shop is optimized for mobile users, as many TikTok viewers will be accessing your shop from their smartphones. Use high-quality images, clear product descriptions, and a straightforward navigation system to enhance the shopping experience.

Offer incentives such as discounts, free shipping, or limited-time offers to encourage TikTok viewers to make a purchase. Highlight these incentives in your TikTok videos and CTAs to create a sense of urgency and drive conversions.

Consider implementing a loyalty program to reward repeat customers. Offer exclusive discounts, early access to new products, or special promotions for loyal customers. This not only encourages repeat purchases but also fosters a sense of loyalty and community around your brand.

Analyzing and Refining Your Strategy

Regularly analyzing your performance is essential for continuous improvement. Use TikTok analytics to track the effectiveness of your content, CTAs, and promotions. Identify which videos drive the most traffic to your Etsy shop and analyze what makes them successful.

On your Etsy shop, track key metrics such as conversion rates, average order value, and customer retention rates. Use this data to identify areas for improvement and optimize your shop's performance.

Experiment with different content formats, CTAs, and promotional strategies to see what drives the best results. Continuously refine your approach based on your findings to maximize your conversion rates.

Building Long-Term Relationships

Building long-term relationships with your customers is key to sustained success. Focus on providing excellent customer service, from the moment they land on your Etsy shop to the delivery of their purchase. Address any issues promptly and professionally to maintain a high level of customer satisfaction.

Stay connected with your customers by encouraging them to follow you on TikTok and other social media platforms. Share updates, new product launches, and special promotions to keep them engaged and informed.

Create a sense of community around your brand by regularly featuring customer testimonials, user-generated content, and behind-the-scenes glimpses of your creative process. Show appreciation for your customers' support and involve them in your brand's journey.

Integrating TikTok content with your Etsy listings is a powerful strategy for driving sales and building a loyal customer base. By creating engaging, relevant content on TikTok and seamlessly linking it to your Etsy shop, you can guide viewers from interest to purchase with ease. Regularly analyze your performance and refine your approach to ensure continued success. Embrace the dynamic nature of TikTok, stay responsive to your audience's needs, and enjoy the creative process as you build a thriving presence on this exciting platform.

SHOWCASING PRODUCT FEATURES AND BENEFITS

Imagine your TikTok account as a vibrant marketplace stall, bustling with curious visitors eager to discover what you have to offer. The key to turning these visitors into loyal customers lies in how effectively you showcase your product features and benefits. Each TikTok video is an opportunity to highlight what makes your products unique, useful, and desirable.

To start, focus on clarity and visual appeal. Your videos should quickly capture attention and clearly convey the key features of your products. Use high-quality visuals and engaging narration to walk your audience through what sets your items apart. If you're selling handmade soap, for instance, create a video that shows the process of making the soap, highlighting the natural ingredients, the craftsmanship involved, and the benefits of using a handmade product over a mass-produced one.

Storytelling is a powerful tool in showcasing product features and benefits. Rather than just listing features, weave them into a narrative that resonates with your audience. Share stories about the inspiration behind your products, the problems they solve, and the joy they bring to your customers. For example, if you sell handcrafted jewelry, tell the story of how a particular piece was inspired by a beautiful sunset you witnessed or a cultural heritage you're passionate about preserving. This not only makes your product more relatable but also creates an emotional connection with your audience.

Demonstration videos are particularly effective in showcasing how your products work and the benefits they offer. Show your products in action and provide practical tips on how to use them. For instance, if you sell kitchen gadgets, create videos demonstrating their use in everyday cooking scenarios.

Highlight how they simplify tasks, save time, or improve the cooking experience. This approach not only educates your audience but also convinces them of the product's value.

Incorporate user-generated content to add authenticity and social proof to your product showcases. Encourage your customers to share videos of themselves using your products and feature these on your TikTok profile. Seeing real people enjoying and benefiting from your products can significantly influence potential buyers. It shows that your products are loved and trusted by others, making new customers more likely to take the plunge.

Address common questions and concerns in your videos. Think about the hesitations your potential customers might have and proactively provide answers. For example, if you sell skincare products, create a series of videos addressing frequently asked questions about ingredients, usage, and results. By providing this information upfront, you help build trust and make the purchasing decision easier for your audience.

Visuals are incredibly important in highlighting product benefits. Use close-ups and different angles to show the details and quality of your products. If you're selling clothing, show how the fabric moves and drapes. If it's a piece of furniture, highlight the craftsmanship and materials used. The more detailed and vivid your visuals, the more your audience can appreciate the value of your products.

Consider creating a recurring series that focuses on different products or aspects of your products. For example, a "Feature Friday" where you showcase a different product each week, diving deep into its features, benefits, and customer testimonials. This not only keeps your content fresh and engaging but also gives each product the spotlight it deserves.

Integrating TikTok's features, like duets and stitches, can also enhance your product showcases. Use these tools to create interactive and collaborative content. For instance, stitch a customer's review video with your own demonstration, adding more context and detail about the product they're reviewing. This kind of content is engaging and provides a well-rounded view of your products.

USING TIKTOK STORIES FOR PROMOTIONS

TikTok Stories are a relatively new feature but offer a fantastic way to keep your audience engaged with fresh, ephemeral content. Stories can be used to share updates, behind-the-scenes looks, flash sales, and limited-time offers, creating a sense of urgency and exclusivity that can drive immediate action.

Start by using Stories to give your audience a behind-the-scenes look at your business. Share glimpses of your workspace, the process of making your products, and the daily life of your brand. This transparency builds a deeper connection with your audience, making them feel like they're part of your journey. For example, if you run a handmade candle business, share Stories of you mixing scents, pouring wax, and packaging orders. These snippets of authenticity make your brand more relatable and trustworthy.

Flash sales and limited-time offers are perfect for TikTok Stories. The temporary nature of Stories creates a natural urgency that encourages quick action. Announce a flash sale exclusively for your TikTok followers, offering a discount or a special deal that's only available for 24 hours. Use clear, compelling CTAs like "Swipe up to shop now!" or "Only available today!" to drive traffic to your Etsy shop. Highlight the benefits of acting quickly, such as limited stock or special pricing.

Engage your audience with interactive content in your Stories. Use polls, Q&A sessions, and countdowns to create a two-way interaction. Ask your followers what products they'd like to see next, what colors they prefer, or which designs they love most. This not only provides valuable feedback but also makes your audience feel valued and involved in your brand's decision-making process. For instance, if you're planning a new product launch, use a poll to let your followers vote on their favorite design. Announce the winning design in your Stories, creating excitement and anticipation for its release.

Promote new product launches and restocks through Stories. Share sneak peeks and teasers to build anticipation. For example, if you're about to release a new jewelry collection, post Stories showing close-ups of the pieces, the inspiration behind the designs, and the craftsmanship involved.

Announce the launch date and time, and remind your followers to set their alarms. On the day of the launch, use Stories to count down to the release and share a direct link to the new collection on your Etsy shop.

Customer testimonials and reviews are powerful content for Stories. Share snippets of positive feedback, highlighting the customer's experience and satisfaction. For instance, post a Story with a quote from a five-star review, accompanied by a video of the product in use. This not only builds trust but also provides social proof that can persuade potential buyers.

Use Stories to create a narrative around your promotions. Rather than just posting a sale announcement, craft a story that leads up to it. Share the inspiration behind the sale, the preparation process, and the excitement building up to the event. For example, if you're hosting a holiday sale, start with Stories about your favorite holiday traditions, the inspiration for your holiday-themed products, and behind-the-scenes looks at preparing for the sale. This narrative approach makes your promotion more engaging and memorable.

Highlight user-generated content in your Stories to build a sense of community and encourage more customers to share their experiences. Repost videos of customers unboxing their orders, using your products, or sharing their feedback. Tag the customers and thank them for their support. This not only provides social proof but also makes your customers feel appreciated and valued.

Consistency is key with Stories. Make it a habit to post regularly, keeping your audience engaged and informed. Use a mix of content types—behind-the-scenes looks, promotions, interactive content, and customer testimonials—to keep your Stories varied and interesting. Track the performance of your Stories through TikTok analytics to understand what resonates most with your audience and adjust your strategy accordingly.

By showcasing your product features and benefits effectively and leveraging TikTok Stories for promotions, you can create a compelling and dynamic presence on TikTok that drives traffic to your Etsy shop. Engage your audience with authentic, valuable content and use interactive, time-sensitive Stories to create a sense of urgency and excitement. The combination of these strategies will not only enhance your TikTok engagement but also boost your Etsy sales, turning your TikTok presence into a powerful driver of your business's growth.

CHAPTER 13: ADVANCED TIKTOK TECHNIQUES FOR ETSY SELLERS

USING USER-GENERATED CONTENT

Imagine the joy of seeing your customers share their happiness and satisfaction with your products. This is the essence of user-generated content (UGC). For Etsy sellers, leveraging UGC on TikTok can create a powerful connection with your audience, build trust, and drive sales.

User-generated content includes any form of content—videos, images, reviews, or testimonials—created by your customers. When your customers share their experiences with your products, it acts as a genuine endorsement. People trust other people more than they trust brands, making UGC incredibly valuable.

To begin using UGC effectively, encourage your customers to share their experiences with your products on TikTok. You can do this by including a note in your packaging that asks them to share a video and tag your account. Offer an incentive, like a discount on their next purchase, for those who post a review or a video using your products. This small gesture can generate a lot of authentic content that showcases your products in real-world settings.

When customers tag your account or use your branded hashtag, take the opportunity to engage with their content. Comment on their posts, thank them for their support, and share their videos on your profile. This not only acknowledges their contribution but also fosters a sense of community. For instance, if a customer shares a video of them unboxing one of your handmade candles, comment on the video to express your gratitude and excitement. Repost the video on your profile to show other followers that real people love and use your products.

User-generated content can also be strategically integrated into your marketing campaigns. Create themed campaigns where you invite your customers to participate. For example, if you sell handmade jewelry, run a campaign where customers share how they style your pieces. Offer a reward for the best video or feature the top entries on your profile. This not only encourages more people to participate but also provides you with a stream of fresh, authentic content that highlights your products.

Another effective approach is to feature customer testimonials in your TikTok videos. Compile snippets of positive reviews or messages from your customers and create a video that showcases their feedback. Overlay these testimonials on videos of your products in action, creating a compelling narrative that combines social proof with visual appeal.

Always seek permission before sharing someone else's content. Reach out to the customer, thank them for their support, and ask if you can share their video on your profile. Most customers will be thrilled to be featured and will appreciate your respect for their content.

Engaging with user-generated content goes beyond just reposting videos. Take the time to interact with the creators. Send them a personal thank-you message, offer them an exclusive discount, or even feature them in your stories. This personal touch can turn a one-time customer into a loyal advocate for your brand.

By showcasing user-generated content, you build trust and authenticity. Potential customers can see real people enjoying your products, which can greatly influence their purchasing decisions. It creates a sense of community and belonging, making your brand more relatable and trustworthy.

CHAPTER 14: EXPANDING YOUR REACH BEYOND TIKTOK

CROSS-PROMOTING ON OTHER SOCIAL MEDIA PLATFORMS

Imagine you've built a bustling market stall on TikTok, drawing in curious customers with your engaging content and unique products. Now, it's time to set up similar stalls across other platforms, inviting even more visitors to discover and fall in love with what you offer. Cross-promoting on other social media platforms is like planting seeds in various fertile grounds, allowing your brand to grow and thrive in different spaces.

Each social media platform has its unique culture, audience, and content style. To effectively cross-promote, it's essential to understand these nuances and tailor your content accordingly. Let's explore how you can strategically expand your reach across various platforms while maintaining a cohesive brand identity.

Start with Instagram, a visual-centric platform that complements TikTok well. On Instagram, your beautifully crafted images and short videos can captivate an audience that appreciates aesthetics and inspiration. Use Instagram Stories to share snippets of your TikTok content, giving your followers a taste of what they can find on your TikTok profile. For example, share a 15-second clip of a popular TikTok video in your Story, adding a swipe-up link (if available) or a clear call-to-action to visit your TikTok for the full video.

Instagram Reels is another excellent tool for cross-promotion. Reels allow you to create short, engaging videos similar to TikTok, making it easy to repurpose your TikTok content. Share your best-performing TikTok videos as Reels, ensuring they fit within Instagram's vertical format and duration limits. Use relevant hashtags and engaging captions to attract new followers and drive traffic back to your TikTok and Etsy shop.

Facebook, with its extensive reach and diverse user base, offers another opportunity for cross-promotion. Create a dedicated Facebook Page for your brand where you share updates, product launches, and behind-the-scenes content. Use Facebook Stories to repurpose your TikTok videos, and consider hosting Facebook Live sessions to engage with your audience in real time. Join relevant Facebook Groups where potential customers gather and share your TikTok content and Etsy shop links when appropriate. This not only drives traffic but also establishes you as an active and valuable member of these communities.

Twitter, known for its real-time updates and concise content, can be an effective platform for quick promotions and engagement. Share links to your TikTok videos with intriguing captions that entice followers to click and watch. Use Twitter to announce new TikTok content, product launches, and special promotions, creating a sense of urgency and excitement. Engage with your Twitter followers by responding to their comments and retweeting their content, fostering a sense of community and loyalty.

Pinterest, a visual discovery platform, can be particularly powerful for driving traffic to your Etsy shop. Create pins featuring your products, linking directly to your Etsy listings. Use Pinterest Boards to organize your pins by themes, such as "Handmade Jewelry" or "Home Decor Ideas." Share your TikTok videos as Idea Pins, giving Pinterest users a glimpse of your content and encouraging them to follow you on TikTok for more inspiration.

LinkedIn, primarily a professional networking site, can be useful if your products or services appeal to businesses or professionals. Share your TikTok content on LinkedIn to showcase your expertise, creativity, and business journey. Write engaging posts that tell the story behind your brand, highlight your achievements, and share valuable insights. This can attract potential business partners, collaborators, and customers who appreciate your entrepreneurial spirit.

Snapchat, with its focus on short-lived, engaging content, can be another avenue for cross-promotion. Share snippets of your TikTok videos as Snapchat Stories, and encourage your

Snapchat followers to check out your full videos on TikTok. Use Snapchat to offer exclusive behind-the-scenes content, sneak peeks of upcoming products, and flash sales, creating a sense of exclusivity and urgency.

While cross-promoting, consistency in your brand voice and visuals is crucial. Ensure that your profile pictures, bios, and overall aesthetics are cohesive across all platforms. This creates a recognizable brand identity, making it easy for your audience to connect with you, regardless of the platform they're using.

EMAIL MARKETING TIPS

While social media is powerful, email marketing remains a vital tool for building a deeper relationship with your audience. It allows you to communicate directly with your customers, providing them with personalized content and exclusive offers. Let's explore how you can harness the power of email marketing to drive traffic to your Etsy shop and keep your customers engaged.

Start by building a robust email list. Encourage your TikTok and social media followers to subscribe to your newsletter by offering an incentive, such as a discount on their first purchase or access to exclusive content. Promote your email sign-up form on your social media profiles, website, and Etsy shop. Make the sign-up process simple and user-friendly to maximize conversions.

Segment your email list to send targeted and relevant content to different groups of subscribers. For example, you might have segments for new subscribers, repeat customers, or those who have shown interest in specific product categories. Tailoring your emails to these segments ensures that your content resonates with each group, increasing engagement and conversion rates.

Craft compelling subject lines that capture your subscribers' attention and entice them to open your emails. Use personalization, urgency, and curiosity to create intrigue. For instance, a subject line like "Just for You: Exclusive Discount on Our Best-Selling Jewelry!" or "Sneak Peek: New Home Decor Collection Launching Tomorrow!" can drive higher open rates.

The content of your emails should be visually appealing, informative, and action-oriented. Use high-quality images of your products, engaging copy that tells the story behind your brand, and clear calls-to-action that guide subscribers to your Etsy shop. Highlight new arrivals, best-sellers, and special promotions to keep your audience excited and engaged.

Leverage the power of storytelling in your emails. Share behind-the-scenes looks at your creative process, customer success stories, and the inspiration behind your products. This not only builds a deeper connection with your audience but also reinforces the authenticity and uniqueness of your brand.

Offer exclusive content and promotions to your email subscribers. This could include early access to new collections, special discounts, or free shipping offers. By providing exclusive perks, you make your subscribers feel valued and appreciated, encouraging loyalty and repeat purchases.

Incorporate user-generated content in your emails to build trust and social proof. Feature customer reviews, testimonials, and photos of customers using your products. This not only validates the quality of your products but also creates a sense of community among your customers.

Use automation to streamline your email marketing efforts. Set up automated welcome emails for new subscribers, abandoned cart reminders, and follow-up emails after a purchase. Automation ensures timely and relevant communication with your subscribers, improving engagement and conversion rates.

Regularly analyze your email marketing performance to understand what works and what doesn't. Track key metrics such as open rates, click-through rates, and conversion rates. Use these insights to optimize your email content, design, and sending times. A/B testing can be particularly useful for experimenting with different subject lines, layouts, and calls-to-action to see what resonates best with your audience.

Email marketing is a powerful way to nurture your audience, build long-term relationships, and drive consistent traffic to your Etsy shop. By delivering valuable, personalized content to your subscribers, you can keep them engaged and motivated to support your brand.

PAID ADVERTISING STRATEGIES

Paid advertising can significantly amplify your reach and accelerate your growth on TikTok and other platforms. When done correctly, it can attract new customers, increase sales, and enhance brand awareness. Let's explore some effective paid advertising strategies that can help you achieve these goals.

TikTok offers various advertising options, including in-feed ads, branded hashtag challenges, and TopView ads. In-feed ads are short videos that appear in users' feeds, blending seamlessly with organic content. These ads can be highly engaging, especially when they are creative, authentic, and aligned with TikTok's casual and entertaining vibe. To create effective in-feed ads, focus on storytelling, use catchy visuals and music, and include a strong call-to-action that directs viewers to your Etsy shop.

Branded hashtag challenges encourage user participation and can generate a lot of engagement and user-generated content. Create a challenge that is fun, easy to participate in, and relevant to your brand. For example, if you sell handmade clothing, you could start a challenge where participants showcase their outfits styled with your pieces. Promote the challenge with sponsored content and use influencers to kick-start participation.

TopView ads are premium placements that appear when users open the TikTok app. These full-screen ads are highly visible and can deliver a strong impact. Use this format to showcase your best products, highlight special promotions, or tell your brand story in a captivating way. The key is to grab attention immediately with compelling visuals and a clear, enticing message.

Beyond TikTok, consider using Facebook and Instagram ads to reach a broader audience. These platforms offer advanced targeting options, allowing you to reach potential customers based on demographics, interests, and behaviors. Create visually appealing ads that align with the aesthetic of each platform. Use carousel ads to showcase multiple products, video ads to tell your brand story, and collection ads to provide a seamless shopping experience within the app.

Google Ads can help you capture search traffic from people actively looking for products like yours. Use Google Shopping ads to display your products directly in search results, complete with images, prices, and links to your Etsy shop. Optimize your product listings with relevant keywords to ensure they appear in search queries. Additionally, use Google Display ads to reach potential customers across millions of websites and apps, increasing your brand visibility.

Retargeting ads are an effective way to re-engage visitors who have shown interest in your products but haven't made a purchase. Use retargeting on platforms like Facebook, Instagram, and Google to remind these visitors of your products and encourage them to complete their purchase. Offer a special discount or highlight customer reviews to persuade them to return and buy.

CHAPTER 14: SCALING YOUR ETSY BUSINESS WITH TIKTOK

OUTSOURCING AND HIRING HELP

Imagine your Etsy business as a thriving garden, each product a blooming flower. As your garden flourishes, tending to every plant becomes increasingly challenging. Outsourcing and hiring help are like enlisting skilled gardeners to assist you, ensuring every flower continues to bloom while you focus on overall growth. For an Etsy seller leveraging TikTok, scaling up involves more than just increasing product volume; it requires a strategic approach to manage demand and maintain quality.

Outsourcing starts with identifying the tasks that consume significant time and could be efficiently handled by others. This might include production, order fulfillment, customer service, or social media management. By delegating these tasks, you free up valuable time to focus on strategic planning, product development, and marketing.

Begin with production. If your products are handmade, consider partnering with skilled artisans or small manufacturing units that can maintain your quality standards. Finding the right partner is crucial. Look for individuals or businesses with a track record of quality craftsmanship and reliability. Start by outsourcing a small batch to test their capabilities. This ensures that they can produce to your specifications and meet your quality expectations.

For instance, if you make handmade candles, you could hire an assistant to help with the production process. They can handle tasks like melting the wax, adding fragrances, and pouring the candles into molds. This allows you to focus on creating new scents and designing attractive packaging. Training your assistant thoroughly is essential to ensure consistency and quality in every batch.

Order fulfillment is another area where outsourcing can significantly impact your business efficiency. Partner with a fulfillment service that can handle storage, packing, and shipping of your products. This not only saves time but also ensures that orders are processed quickly and accurately. Look for a fulfillment partner experienced in handling delicate or handmade items, ensuring they can pack and ship your products with care.

Customer service is critical for maintaining a positive reputation. As your business grows, the volume of customer inquiries and issues will likely increase. Hiring a customer service representative to handle emails, messages, and returns can improve your response time and customer satisfaction. Train them to understand your products, brand voice, and customer service standards. This ensures that every customer interaction reflects your brand values and enhances their experience.

Social media management is another area ripe for outsourcing. A dedicated social media manager can help you create and schedule posts, engage with followers, and analyze performance metrics. This ensures a consistent online presence and allows you to focus on other aspects of your business. When hiring a social media manager, look for someone with experience in managing TikTok and other relevant platforms. They should understand the nuances of creating engaging content, leveraging trends, and driving traffic to your Etsy shop.

Outsourcing doesn't mean relinquishing control. Regularly communicate with your team to ensure they understand your vision and standards. Use project management tools to track progress and maintain accountability. Regular check-ins and feedback sessions can help address any issues promptly and keep everyone aligned with your business goals.

EXPANDING PRODUCT LINES

As your Etsy business grows, expanding your product lines can attract new customers and increase sales from existing ones. Think of this as planting new varieties in your garden, each bringing its unique appeal and beauty. Expanding your product range involves both creativity and strategic planning.

Start by analyzing your current products and identifying gaps in the market. Consider what complementary items could enhance your existing offerings. For example, if you sell handmade jewelry, you might expand into accessories like hair clips or scarves that complement your pieces. Listen to customer feedback and requests; their insights can be invaluable in identifying new product opportunities.

Research trends within your niche and broader market. Platforms like Pinterest, Instagram, and TikTok can provide inspiration for new products. Pay attention to what similar brands are offering and how customers are responding. This can help you identify trends early and position your brand as a leader in innovation.

Developing new products requires thorough testing to ensure they meet your quality standards and resonate with your audience. Create prototypes and gather feedback from trusted customers or focus groups. This iterative process helps refine your products before launching them to a broader audience.

Use TikTok to build excitement around your new product launches. Share behind-the-scenes looks at the development process, tease new items, and gather input from your followers. This not only builds anticipation but also makes your audience feel involved in the creation process. For instance, if you're launching a new line of scented candles, share videos of scent testing, packaging design, and the first batch being made. Engage your followers by asking for their input on scent combinations or label designs.

Seasonal and limited-edition products can also drive excitement and urgency. Plan special collections around holidays, seasons, or trends. Limited-edition items create a sense of exclusivity and can drive quick sales. Promote these collections extensively on TikTok, highlighting their unique features and the limited availability.

Collaborations with other creators or brands can further expand your product lines and reach. Partner with influencers, artists, or complementary brands to create co-branded products. This not only introduces your brand to new audiences but also adds a fresh perspective to your product offerings. For example, if you sell home decor, collaborate with a local artist to create a unique collection of hand-painted items.

Managing an expanded product line requires efficient inventory management and forecasting. Use inventory management software to track stock levels, sales trends, and reorder points. This helps ensure you can meet demand without overstocking. Regularly review your sales data to identify top-performing products and potential slow movers.

EXPLORING WHOLESALE OPPORTUNITIES

Expanding into wholesale can significantly scale your Etsy business, introducing your products to a broader market. Think of this as moving from a local farmer's market to supplying several stores, exponentially increasing your reach. Wholesale involves selling your products in bulk to retailers, who then sell them to their customers.

Start by identifying potential wholesale partners. Look for retailers that align with your brand values and target market. These could be local boutiques, specialty shops, or larger retail chains. Research their product offerings and customer base to ensure a good fit. Attend trade shows, industry events, and networking opportunities to connect with potential buyers.

Create a professional wholesale catalog that showcases your products, pricing, and terms. Include high-quality images, detailed descriptions, and information about your brand. Clearly outline your wholesale pricing, minimum order quantities, and payment terms. This catalog serves as a key tool for presenting your products to potential buyers.

Developing a wholesale strategy involves setting competitive pricing that ensures profitability while being attractive to retailers. Calculate your costs, including production, packaging, and shipping, to determine a pricing structure that maintains healthy margins. Consider offering volume discounts or incentives for larger orders to encourage bulk purchases.

Pitch your products to potential wholesale buyers with confidence and clarity. Prepare a compelling pitch that highlights the unique features and benefits of your products, your brand story, and your track record of customer satisfaction. Reach out to retailers with personalized emails, send them samples, and follow up with a phone call or meeting.

Leverage TikTok to build your wholesale presence. Share content that highlights your wholesale capabilities, such as behind-the-scenes looks at production, packaging large orders, or testimonials from existing wholesale partners. Use TikTok to announce your participation in trade shows or industry events, inviting potential buyers to visit your booth.

Building strong relationships with wholesale partners is crucial for long-term success. Provide excellent customer service, timely communication, and reliable order fulfillment. Offer marketing support, such as high-quality images and promotional materials, to help them sell your products effectively. Regularly check in with your wholesale partners to gather feedback and address any issues.

Consider creating a dedicated section on your website or Etsy shop for wholesale inquiries. Provide detailed information about your wholesale program, including how to apply, order minimums, and contact details. This makes it easy for interested retailers to learn more and reach out to you.

Exploring wholesale opportunities can transform your business, providing steady, large-volume orders and introducing your brand to new markets. It requires careful planning, strategic pricing, and strong relationship management, but the potential rewards are significant.

CONCLUSION

YOUR JOURNEY TO SIX FIGURES AND BEYOND

As you stand at the threshold of transforming your Etsy business with the power of TikTok, imagine the journey you've embarked upon. You've planted seeds in the fertile ground of creativity and dedication, nurtured them with strategic planning and hard work, and now, you watch as they bloom into a thriving garden of success. Your journey to six figures and beyond is not just about numbers; it's about growth, learning, and the unwavering pursuit of your passion.

Picture the first time you uploaded a TikTok video, filled with excitement and a bit of uncertainty. You wondered how your handmade products would be received in this vast digital landscape. But as the views started to climb and the likes and comments poured in, you realized that TikTok wasn't just another social media platform. It was a vibrant community where creativity and authenticity were celebrated, where you could share your story and connect with people who appreciated your craft.

Every step of your journey has been a learning experience. From understanding the intricacies of TikTok's algorithm to mastering the art of engaging content, you've adapted and grown. You've discovered the power of user-generated content, seeing firsthand how your customers' stories can amplify your brand's reach and credibility. You've hosted exciting giveaways and contests, turning passive viewers into active participants and loyal customers.

Your journey has also involved smart outsourcing and hiring, allowing you to focus on what you do best while trusted partners handle the rest. Whether it's production, order fulfillment, or customer service, you've built a team that supports your vision and helps you scale efficiently. Expanding your product lines has brought new excitement and diversity to your offerings, while exploring wholesale opportunities has opened doors to broader markets and steady, large-volume orders.

But this journey is far from over. As you continue to grow and evolve, there are always new strategies to explore, new trends to leverage, and new connections to make. The world of TikTok and e-commerce is dynamic and ever-changing, offering endless possibilities for those who dare to dream and innovate.

FINAL TIPS AND ENCOURAGEMENT

As you forge ahead, here are some final tips to keep you motivated and on track:

1. Stay True to Your Brand: Authenticity is your greatest asset. Your unique story, your passion, and your dedication are what set you apart. Stay true to your brand's identity and values, and let them shine through in everything you do.

2. Keep Learning and Adapting: The digital landscape is constantly evolving. Stay curious and open to new ideas. Continuously educate yourself about the latest trends, tools, and strategies. Adapt to changes and be willing to experiment and take risks.

3. Engage with Your Community: Your customers and followers are the heart of your business. Engage with them genuinely and consistently. Listen to their feedback, appreciate their support, and make them feel valued. A strong, engaged community is a powerful driver of growth and success.

4. Invest in Quality: Whether it's your products, your content, or your customer service, always strive for quality. High standards build trust and loyalty, ensuring that customers return and recommend you to others.

5. Balance Creativity and Strategy: Creativity fuels your passion and innovation, but strategy ensures sustainability and growth. Find a balance between the two. Plan strategically while allowing room for creative exploration and spontaneity.

6. Celebrate Milestones: Take time to celebrate your achievements, no matter how small. Each milestone is a testament to your hard work and dedication. Celebrate with your team and your community, sharing your joy and gratitude.

RESOURCES FOR ONGOING SUPPORT

Your journey doesn't end here. As you continue to scale your Etsy business with TikTok, numerous resources can provide ongoing support and guidance. Here are some valuable resources to consider:

1. TikTok Business Resources: TikTok offers a wealth of resources for businesses, including tutorials, best practices, and success stories. Explore the TikTok for Business website and their Creator Portal for tips on creating engaging content and leveraging TikTok's features.

2. Etsy Seller Handbook: The Etsy Seller Handbook is a comprehensive guide to running a successful Etsy shop. It covers everything from shop policies and SEO to marketing and customer service. Regularly check for updates and new articles to stay informed.

3. Online Courses and Webinars: Invest in online courses and webinars that focus on e-commerce, digital marketing, and social media strategies. Platforms like Udemy, Coursera, and Skillshare offer courses that can enhance your skills and knowledge.

Follow industry blogs and podcasts to stay updated on the latest trends and insights. Blogs like HubSpot, Shopify, and Social Media Examiner offer valuable content for e-commerce businesses. Podcasts such as "The Side Hustle School" and "Etsy Conversations" provide inspiration and practical advice from successful entrepreneurs.

5. Networking and Support Groups: Join networking groups and support communities where you can connect with fellow Etsy sellers and e-commerce entrepreneurs. Online forums, Facebook groups, and local meetups offer opportunities to share experiences, seek advice, and build valuable relationships.

6. Analytics and Tools: Utilize analytics tools to track your performance and make data-driven decisions. Tools like Google Analytics, TikTok Analytics, and Etsy's Shop Stats provide insights into your audience, traffic, and sales. Regularly review these metrics to understand what's working and where you can improve.

7. Mentorship and Coaching: Consider seeking mentorship or coaching from experienced entrepreneurs and industry experts. A mentor can provide personalized guidance, support, and accountability as you navigate the challenges of scaling your business.

Your journey to six figures and beyond is a testament to your creativity, resilience, and entrepreneurial spirit. Embrace every challenge as an opportunity to learn and grow. Celebrate your successes and continue striving for excellence. With passion, dedication, and the right strategies, the possibilities for your Etsy business are limitless.

As you move forward, remember that the support of your community, the power of authentic storytelling, and the innovative potential of platforms like TikTok are your greatest allies. Keep nurturing your garden of success, and watch as it flourishes and grows, reaching new heights and inspiring others along the way.

Your story is just beginning, and the journey ahead is filled with exciting opportunities and adventures. Embrace it with confidence, curiosity, and a heart full of passion. The world is waiting to see what you'll create next.

Printed in Great Britain
by Amazon